Katrina's Story

Katrina's Story

Katrina Leeder

as told to Tom Haslock

GRANADA
MEDIA

First published in Great Britain in 1999
by Granada Media, an imprint of André Deutsch Ltd
76 Dean Street
London W1V 5HA
www.vci.co.uk

Katrina Leeder and Tom Haslock are the joint authors of this work
respectively and have asserted their right under the Copyright, Designs and
Patents Act 1988 to be identified as the joint authors of this work.

A catalogue record for this title is available from the British Library

ISBN 0 233 99769 5

Typeset by
Derek Doyle & Associates, Liverpool
Printed and bound by
Mackays of Chatham

1 3 5 7 9 10 8 6 4 2

This book is dedicated to past, present and future cancer sufferers. Beat the cancer, don't let the cancer beat you.

Contents

Acknowledgements

I would like to thank:

My mum for helping, guiding, encouraging, supporting and showering me with love all through my illness.

My darling husband, Julian, for never doubting me, standing by me and accepting me for who I am.

The rest of my family for the love, support and encouragement shown to me.

Our vicar, Ruth Matthews, for marrying us in her church.

Everybody involved with the wedding preparations before and during our wedding day because without your help the wedding would not have been possible.

Blenheim ward for making our wedding night a memorable one.

My surgeons, my consultant and her radiotherapy team.

CLIC House for letting myself, Mum or Julian stay during my radiotherapy treatment.

All the medical staff who have helped care for me during my illness.

Reed Aviation for supporting me throughout my illness and supporting me while returning to work.

Waitrose for allowing Julian to take time off to be with me.

The general public for the letters of support that have been sent to me.

Introduction

I was married to Julian Batham in August 1998, a day of hectic activity, reunion with family and friends, laughter, tears, happy memories of the past and many concerned thoughts about the future.

A normal wedding day, one of thousands that must have taken place that weekend, special only to those who were taking part. Special to me, to Julian, to Mum and Dad, to everyone who was there for those few precious hours.

But it was also special to thirteen million other people who, unnoticed by us and unseen by us at the time, watched with a lump in their throats and many a soggy tissue as, a few months after the great event, our private wedding was broadcast on national TV.

Why my wedding?

Why me?

That is the question I have asked myself many times, and to which I have never found an answer. All I can tell is the story as it unfolded around me, sweeping me along.

PART ONE
1990–92

Chapter 1

It all began at another wedding several years earlier, my brother Darren's in July 1990.

I was still at school, still growing up, and I was going to be one of the bridesmaids for Suzanne, his bride.

On the big day I went round in the morning to Darren's house to put on the dress, and for some reason we couldn't get it to do up. We all laughed, because I was just about the last person to be putting on weight. No one could understand what had happened. I looked well, I felt well, and I was fit and slim. We had to assume that the seamstress had made a mistake somehow.

Only a month before I had had the dress fitted, and of course it went on me perfectly then. Not now, though. We pulled at it, and tried to let out seams, but there really wasn't time to make it fit properly.

When it was obvious nothing could be done, I had to make a switch with one of the other bridesmaids; she wore my dress and I wore hers. I looked good enough in her dress, but I think mine was a little too short for her. Still, no one really looks too closely at the bridesmaids on a wedding day, and no one would have noticed anything was wrong.

But that was when I realized I was starting to grow. The date was 21 July 1990, a day I thought I was always going to remember because it was Darren and Suzanne's big day. Now it has acquired a different significance for me. I thought no more about it at the time and the weeks slipped by normally for a while.

Five months later, in the days before Christmas 1990, I wasn't feeling so good. I couldn't put my finger on it. I had a constant feeling of tiredness, a general feeling that I was going to be sick. I said nothing of it to anyone else: I assumed it was something to do with growing pains, with work at school, with not getting enough sleep, with something that must be bothering me.

I hated feeling sick, dreaded throwing up. This had always been true, ever since I was tiny. So extreme was my hatred of it that I would stay away from any activity that looked likely to upset me. For instance, I used to avoid the most extreme rides whenever I went to a fairground.

But all through November of that year, then increasingly as Christmas approached, I was fighting back a feeling that I was going to be ill. When I got up in the morning I would go to the bathroom and clean my teeth, but then as soon as I put the toothbrush in my mouth I would heave as if I was going to be sick. I would stare into the mirror at myself, feeling faint, wondering what was going on.

I had always been reluctant to get out of bed in the

mornings – particularly at weekends, and more particularly on recent weekends when I had sometimes felt so rough I'd stay in bed most of the days – but now I found myself putting off this first bathroom visit for as long as possible. What was happening to me?

In spite of this chronic feeling of illness I was working as hard as ever. I had always taken a pride in my school-work and spent hours on homework. I would sometimes stay up to half-past two or three o'clock in the morning to finish it. I made sure there were no spelling mistakes, no errors, that I'd written the work out as neatly as possible.

With that done I would set the alarm for five or six o'clock the next morning. It was always the same: Mum and Dad would say to me, 'Katrina, you know, you really ought to do your work at school. You shouldn't keep bringing this much work home with you.'

What I knew was that at school I didn't take things in first time around. I preferred to take the material home to analyse the subject and think about it in my own time without distractions around me. On top of this, home-work would normally take me ages simply because I was a perfectionist. I liked to make sure it was accurate. I went over everything repeatedly. I'd rather re-write the whole thing than let sloppy work go in for marking.

Then came one particular night. I was working late again, my bedside light still burning in the small hours. At about half-past two Mum came into the room and said, 'Come on, darling. You must get to bed now.'

I had just then managed to finish my English essay

and so I folded up my books and went to bed. I slept normally. But morning came and I felt really ill again.

Mum said to me, 'Why don't you take the day off school?'

Time off school was something I never took. Even as a small child, even when I was really ill, I'd pull on my clothes and gamely go to school. I disliked admitting I wasn't well. I still can't recall being away from school for more than a day or two. I knew the school kept an attendance record, and I was proud that mine was really good.

So that day I told Mum, 'No, no . . . I'll go to school.'

I did, but from the moment I arrived, everyone I saw began remarking on how washed-out and grey I looked. They said they thought I wasn't getting enough sleep, that I was coming down with something. I couldn't deny it: I knew something was wrong with me. I was a long way from being my best – that endless sense of tiredness, the terrible, nagging feeling that I was about to be sick.

I was on my way up to my German lesson, which was in a classroom at the top of a long flight of stairs, when the dizziness suddenly grew much worse. I put out a hand to open the door, but I never made it. I turned around, swayed, and everything went black around me. I was right at the top of the stairs and if my friends hadn't been there to catch me I would have fallen down to the bottom.

I came round in the nurse's room, resting on the couch in the half dark. The nurse telephoned home then contacted my GP. I lay still, waiting for Dad to come and collect me.

The doctor saw me soon after we arrived at the surgery, and conducted an examination while Dad sat anxiously by. He took a blood test.

A few days later he rang to say that the blood count was extremely low, and that he was going to put me on iron medicine for three months. We went to the chemist and collected a massive brown bag containing the bottles. At this point I was still in no pain.

A week later I was feeling worse. I'd been taking the medicine regularly, and although the doctor had warned us that we shouldn't expect much improvement within one week, we certainly hadn't expected the situation to deteriorate. My parents took me back to the doctor. He did another blood test and warned us that he thought the results might mean I would have to be hospitalized.

Two days later the doctor rang Mum at work. He said the blood count was even worse and that I was running on practically nothing. He told my mum he was sending an ambulance to take me to hospital immediately. By this time I no longer had enough energy even to get out of bed. My parents knew I didn't like ambulances, so they took me themselves in the car. I was beginning to realize it must be serious.

A short time later I was in Casualty at the local hospital. After a short wait I was taken to a small room to one side and I lay down on the bed there. I was to be in there for ages while a succession of doctors came round to see me and examine me. One by one they trooped in, said hello, then began to feel and examine my stomach. My mum remained with me the whole time – a great support.

I was worried through all this, but genuinely had no inkling of what was going on, what might be concerning them, what they thought my illness could be. I knew that my stomach had been swollen back in the summer at the time of Darren's wedding, that it had grown slightly since then, but the main symptoms that bothered me were still those familiar but unpleasant feelings of fatigue and sickness.

Then came the moment when the long sequence of nasty shocks began.

One doctor felt my stomach with his hands, pressing it gently but firmly, inching his way across it. Then he listened, slowly and carefully, with his stethoscope. Finally, he removed the scope from his ears, and looked at me in a puzzled way.

'Is there a chance you might be pregnant?' he asked.

I said immediately, 'No.'

I was amazed by the question.

The doctor frowned and listened again to my stomach. I noticed Mum moving a little closer to me.

'I'm not pregnant,' I said. 'How could I be?'

'I know you're not pregnant, darling,' she said at once.

I was sixteen and all I had ever done with a boy was hold hands. But the doctor didn't seem able to believe me.

'Tell him, Mum.'

'Katrina wouldn't lie about this,' she said to him straight away. 'I know her too well.'

That night they put me into a general ward and I sent mum home with a list of the clothes I would like. At this time I actually thought I'd be in hospital only a couple of days – two or three days at the most.

It was 6 December 1990, a date I was never going to forget.

Chapter 2

I'd gone to the doctor's that week to get the results of a blood test, and here I was in the medical ward of the local hospital with something inside me.

Earlier in the day my dad had gone to school to collect my new school photograph. I still have it now, of course, but it was with me that night in hospital. It had been taken only a month before, a picture of me in my school uniform, with my long blonde hair. It was propped up on the table beside my bed together with one of my cuddly toys; a glimpse of home, of my real life, my real identity. That identity had nothing to do with this.

It was eleven o'clock at night by the time they had found me a place in the ward and wheeled me down there. It was late, really late, but as soon as I was there they gave me a blood transfusion.

I think techniques have improved and modernized since then, but that first time what they gave me was little more than a drip feeding in gradually from a bottle-shaped bag. The blood dripped extremely slowly into my veins. After a while I started getting spasms and

I'd go into shock. My arm would shake and I was in continual pain all through that night. The transfusions went on and on: no sooner was one bag of blood taken off the stand than another one appeared, and then another ... It was a long night for me, with precious little sleep.

In the morning my mum turned up at hospital, having taken the day off work. I had to go for an ultrasound scan and she came with me. The ultrasound technician completed her tests, then I was taken back to the ward.

What followed was to create and shape one of the most difficult of my experiences.

Obviously, at this point the medical staff knew what they had found. They must have known immediately that it was a cancerous tumour. However, I was in everyone's eyes just a child, a young girl in her midteens. Was I to be told? Not straight away, they decided. Instead, they told my mum.

The doctor came to the ward and asked to speak to Mum outside. Obviously, I didn't hear what was said, but from what happened afterwards I was able to piece together the gist of it.

He would have said, 'Mrs Leeder, we are certain that Katrina has a tumour, and that it is likely to be malignant. Before we can go any further we must establish what kind of cancer it is.'

'Have you told her?' Mum would have said.

'No – this is what I need to ask you. Do you want Katrina to know?'

Can you imagine any worse question a mother might ever have to face? Many times I have tried to imagine what Mum must have gone through that day, and on many others that were to follow. This revelation would have come to her as a thunderbolt, the most terrible news of all.

Your daughter has cancer. She will probably die.

But more than that, Mum was being asked to decide if I should be told. In some ways, my mum knows me better than I know myself. We have the closest of relationships, a level of total trust in each other. She knew at that moment something that even I have difficulty accepting.

She knew that if she or anyone else was to say those coldest of words to me – 'You have cancer' – then I would think of only one thing: death.

Cancer is death. The two words were always linked.

When you heard the word being used, on television for example, it was always bad news. Somebody had died from it. Someone else had it and wasn't expected to survive. You never heard about those who had survived it. Maybe it is a terrible thing for me to admit this, but that is how it was. Cancer was death.

Mum undoubtedly knew this. She knew me, how I would react, and in almost every important way she was right.

Mum would have said to that doctor, 'Look, to be honest, I don't think you can come straight out with those words: "You have cancer." I think the only way to approach it would be to say to Katrina, "You have a tumour." And hopefully she will say, "Does that mean I've got cancer?" That would allow her to approach the subject her own way.'

I knew none of this at the time. All I knew was that they had found something weird and unpleasant in my stomach and that they were outside the ward discussing me.

In a moment I saw the doctor returning. He came up to the bed and he said, 'Look, Katrina, I just need to let you know what we've found. What you have is a tumour.'

I hadn't the faintest idea at that time what that meant.

'Oh, what is a tumour?' I said innocently.

'It's a big mass of cells,' he said. 'It grows together.'

And yet even though I didn't understand everything, I knew somehow that it wasn't what I had wanted him to say. It wasn't definite enough. I must have sensed something was being kept back from me.

He was still talking.

'We need to do a test called a biopsy,' he said. 'We have to find out what type of tumour it is you are carrying. Then we will know the best way to treat it.'

That's how it was left. They said I had a tumour, but they didn't even know what kind it was.

A little later I was taken down to the operating theatre for them to extract some cells from the tumour. The doctor allowed Mum to come into the theatre with me. At this point I discovered that you are treated differently according to how old you are and how they interpret that.

I was sixteen years old. Everyone who has been sixteen knows what a difficult age it can be: you want to be grown up, but you can't entirely throw off the habits of childhood. Now I was in an institution where this confusion was actually built into the rules. In some respects they classed me as an adult; in others I was treated as still being a child. It might seem a fine distinction to anyone reading this, but I was to learn the hard way that it was going to have a crucial impact on my treatment.

For the time being they were deciding to treat me as an adult. I was sixteen, so I was grown up. It meant that I wouldn't be given a general anaesthetic for the biopsy. All I had was a local – they numbed my side – and I was put under heavy sedation.

They injected the left side of my body and I was turned over so that I lay on one side, covered by a big green cloth. There was a little hole in this where the first incision would be made. The surgeon was trying to be nice to me, and obviously saw that I was in a bit of a state. To help me relax he put on a tape of slow songs, with titles like 'Nights in White Satin' and 'Don't It Make Your Brown Eyes Blue'.

That helped a bit, but only by distracting me temporarily. I was much more concerned with what he was doing, probably more concerned than he wanted. He was working with what looked to me like a big long skewer, at least a foot long, a kind of semi-flexible rod which he was inserting into me through the incision. On the tip of this skewer was a kind of extracting device.

Obviously this thing was intended to go poking around inside me, and slice off or grab some of whatever was growing there.

I didn't like to think about that. But no amount of pop music would distract me away from it!

It wasn't a quick process. He kept sliding it in and out, peering at a screen at his side, bending deeply over me. It went on so long that after a while the numbness of the local anaesthetic began to wear off.

'I'm starting to feel this!' I said, in some alarm.

He said, 'Look Katrina, it'll be just a few minutes longer. I've nearly finished.'

'It's *hurting*!'

'I'm sorry. We're nearly there.'

The tape had come to an end and the music was silent, so he asked the nurse to turn over the tape. I'll never forget the next song that came on. It was 'I Had the Time of my Life' from the film *Dirty Dancing*. That title! What was happening to me! If I hadn't been in such pain and discomfort I could have laughed.

The music must have had a beneficial effect on me, if only to keep my mind off the pain, because to my immense relief the surgeon suddenly announced that he had finished.

He said to me, 'Do you want to see what just went inside you?'

He held up the implement, and I got my first good look at the thing. I couldn't help recoiling from its appearance, and from the thoughts it aroused, and the memory of the recent pain it had been causing. No medieval instrument of torture could have had a greater effect on me.

He must have seen the expression on my face, because he added, 'You're one brave lady, Katrina.'

Feeling much the worse for wear, I was taken back on the trolley to the ward and put back in my bed. I stayed in hospital a few more days awaiting the results of the biopsy. Then the consultant came to speak to me and my parents. He came straight to the point, or so it seemed to me at that moment.

'We've found a tumour on Katrina's kidney,' he said, 'so we're going to have to remove it.'

I didn't much like the sound of that, but at least it meant that they knew what to do about it.

'It's not the sort of surgical work we can take on here, in a general hospital,' he went on. 'So I'm going to refer you to the John Radcliffe Hospital in Oxford, where they have a specialist children's unit that deals with this kind of thing. It's by far the best place for you to be.'

'Children's unit?' I said.

'Yes, because of the kind of tumour it is. The specialists there are by far the best people to treat you.'

'But I thought . . .'

I didn't finish. I'd gone through all that agony under a local anaesthetic because they thought I was an adult, and now I was a child again. At least I knew that I was going to be in the hands of experts.

Chapter 3

Soon after I arrived at the John Radcliffe, my new consultant came to see me and my mum. He said they had now completed their diagnostic tests on the material they had removed during the biopsy.

'Katrina, we've found that you have what's known as a Wilms Tumour,' he said in a matter-of-fact voice.

I shook my head, obviously never having heard of it before.

'What does that mean?' I said.

'It's a fairly common type of tumour found in children. A Wilms Tumour is a growth that appears on the kidney. It never grows anywhere else. It usually appears on children under the age of five, and rarely appears on anyone older than that.'

'But I'm sixteen,' I said.

'Yes, of course. It means we can't leave it there. Somehow it's never been detected before, but now we know it's there we'll have to take it out.'

He began to describe the plans he had made, but already my mind was racing off in a number of different directions. What I was suffering from had a name. That was something, surely? It was a common childhood ailment. They knew about it, they knew what to do to put it right. All that was surely good news? I searched his expression for a hint that this might be so, but he was giving nothing away. What he was saying instead should have given me cause for more alarm, but I was not to realize the full extent of that until a little later.

I was with my mum in the room they had allocated me, and a social worker knocked on the door and came in. She introduced herself: she seemed really friendly and nice. What she couldn't have known is that our family has always prided itself on being independent-minded, finding strength in ourselves, not looking for help from strangers. Mum in particular is a proud woman, with justification. As soon as we realized this lady was a social worker, I could sense Mum stiffening up.

She said straight away, 'Look, I'm sorry, but we don't need help from a social worker.'

'I'm simply here to explain what's available to you,' said the lady.

'We never accept charity,' Mum said.

'Things can get complicated for families, and there is a lot of help available . . .'

'I've got a lot on my plate at the moment,' Mum said. 'No offence, but I think we can manage on our own.'

I have much the same outlook as Mum, of course. While they were speaking I was thinking to myself, 'I don't need a social worker. People in trouble go to social workers, and I'm just here in hospital for a few tests.'

Cutting across my thoughts, I heard the social worker say, 'Well, the problem, Mrs Leeder, is that your child has cancer, and with a long illness like that . . .'

It was the first time anyone had said the word in my hearing.

Cancer.

A long illness.

Your child has cancer.

Through the swirling feelings of new terror, I managed to say, 'But I haven't got cancer – the doctor said I have a tumour.'

Mum and the social worker stared at me. I could see my mum's face working, and the social worker glanced hurriedly from her to me, then back again.

Mum said, 'Well, Katrina didn't actually know she had cancer.'

'But I thought . . .' said the social worker, her voice fading with embarrassment.

The only person I could trust was my mother.

I said, 'Mum, have I really got cancer?'

'I'm sorry, darling,' she said straight away. 'We didn't know how to break it to you. I was hoping you would understand that a tumour meant it was cancer, that you would understand it yourself, in your own way.'

'I had no idea!' I said. 'I . . .'

I couldn't think clearly. Sheer fright was flowing through me.

We were all silenced by the revelation that had slipped out so easily. No one knew what to say. The only thing I could think, the straw of hope at which I clutched, was that it might be a joke, a terrible, unfunny joke.

I had thought having a tumour was bad enough. But a tumour was a matter of cells growing, like the doctor had said. It was something they could treat, something they could remove. Until that moment, I'd found a strange comfort in the idea of having an operation. There was something there inside me but they knew what to do about it, knew they would be able to remove it.

I'd told myself a hundred times, 'After the operation I'll be all right.'

Mum and I sat in horrified silence. Why hadn't Mum told me this appalling news herself? But I already knew, or had sensed, the answer to that.

We were still sitting there with the social worker when the dinner lady rang the bell in the corridor outside. This had happened enough times already for a little routine to have grown up between Mum and me: Mum usually went out to collect the food for me. But that day I went myself, because Mum was still talking to the social worker. I clambered down from the bed and headed out into the hallway.

That morning, when the dinner list had come round, I'd ticked off my choice quite eagerly. I think it was a roast, with treacle sponge and custard to follow. In a funny kind of way I had had it at the back of my mind all day, anticipating it. Well, my life had been devastated in the last few minutes, and food was about bottom of the list of things I wanted, but even so I went out quite eagerly. I simply had to get out of the room for a few moments.

The dinner lady didn't recognize me, and asked me my name.

'Katrina Leeder,' I said.

'Oh yes, I know. Katrina. Let me see.' She checked me off on her list, then reached down to get my tray. 'You're up already then?'

'Already?' I said.

'After your operation.'

I explained that I was still having tests, that I hadn't actually had the operation yet. I've got to have chemotherapy first.' I took the tray from her. 'They said something about shrinking the tumour before they operated.'

She looked directly at me.

'How do you feel about your hair, love?' she asked. 'It's so long and lovely. Such a shame.'

'My hair? What's a shame?'

'You know, when you have chemotherapy your hair usually falls out.'

Stunned, I backed away from her and headed towards my room with the tray of now unwanted food. What on earth was she talking about?

She had said, 'Your hair usually falls out.'

'Mum!' I shouted. '*Mum!*'

I hurried down the corridor, panic building up in me. I ran into the room.

'It's untrue, isn't it?' My voice came out in a gasping noise. I was practically screaming.

'What is, darling?'

'Tell me it's untrue! My hair isn't going to fall out!'

Mum was sitting there, still looking shell-shocked after the last conversation. I put down the tray heavily.

'What's the matter, love?' she asked me.

'What the dinner lady just told me!' I said desperately.

'What was that?'

'She said the treatment is going to make me lose my hair!'

I sat down on the side of the bed, waiting for her to say something reassuring. I was expecting, hoping, she would say something like, 'She doesn't know what she's talking about!' or, 'What nonsense!' but instead, the expression on Mum's face remained troubled. Again, I glimpsed some of the torment she must have been going through. She said nothing, and would not meet my gaze.

'Mum. . . ?' I said, practically shouting at her. 'Is there something you're not telling me?'

I saw tears in her eyes.

'Look, Katrina,' she said, after another lengthy pause. 'This is so hard. Nothing in my life has ever been as hard as this. We, I . . . I thought you'd know. They have to use chemo to treat your tumour, but it does have a side-effect. It will probably – no, definitely, it will make you lose your hair. I know what your hair means to you, my darling. I didn't know how to tell you. I was hoping you'd know already. I can't tell you how sorry I am you had to find out like that.'

She said this so simply, without emphasis, that it still did not entirely sink in. My world was shattering around me. If anything, the news about my hair was even worse than what the social worker had blurted out. I'd been growing my hair all my life – sixteen years!

So, irrationally, I found myself thinking: it's another joke, another ghastly, sick joke. I knew my mum would never make that kind of joke, but it was the only hope I had left.

I said, 'Oh, I've got it. This is a bad joke, isn't it?'

'No, darling,' Mum said, shaking her head sadly. 'Katrina, this is not a joke. I'm so sorry.'

I couldn't take it in. I'd just found out I had cancer, and ten minutes after that I discovered I was going to lose my hair. All my life I'd loved and wanted long hair. I always looked after it. I never dyed it, always brushed it carefully, kept it clean, hardly ever put hair bands in it. I was careful about not getting split ends.

We were both crying by now. Between sobs I was trying to explain my fears, and she was trying to tell me why it was so hard for her or anyone to tell me the cruel truths about my illness.

In the end I managed to say, 'Look, Mum, what else are they hiding from me?'

And at last she was able to explain as best she could that it wasn't so much the medical staff hiding things from me, it was she herself. She told me what I already knew, deep down, well buried, that I sometimes ran away from the truth, that the harshness of reality was something I had always preferred to creep up on me in stages.

'I thought I knew what you can and can't cope with,' she said. 'But you had to find out this way – complete strangers, letting it slip out!'

She sobbed again, and we held each other, trying to find what comfort we could. We knew one another so well. Gradually, I realized that if it hadn't been for these chance remarks her strategy would have been the right one.

I knew that if someone – Mum, or one of the doctors or nurses, the dinner lady, anyone else – had come straight out at the beginning and uttered the dread words, I wouldn't have been able to cope. I would have gone completely to pieces. I would have thought, 'I'm going to die.'

When the spirit is crushed, the body finds it so much harder to fight.

I knew that if I had had the opportunity, in advance, to have some say in how I was 'told' about my illness, then I would have given anything not to have found out about it from two complete strangers who simply dropped the cruel information into conversations. What, however, was the alternative? It was mostly my own fault I didn't face up to the truth myself; I therefore believe Mum did take the right approach, even though, in the end, it went so drastically wrong. All this I began to realize as we sat there miserably together.

Eventually, my mum had to leave the room. One of the nurses wanted to talk to her, so she went outside for a while.

I was still upset. I couldn't stop thinking.

Why me?

That is what I asked myself again and again. Why me? Why me? *Why me*? I had never done anything wrong. I had never hurt anyone, never stolen anything, never so much as dropped litter on the ground. Without being a self-conscious goody-goody I had always believed that you should never hurt, never damage, never wreck things for others.

I couldn't understand what was happening to me. It was the worst punishment in the world, a sentence of death. But why? What had I done to deserve it?

In desperation, I tried to think of something, *anything*, I might have done in life that had brought this down on me. It might sound silly now, but there was something. There was one action of mine that always caused trouble at home, was always getting me into hot water. When Mum came back into the room I asked her about it.

I said, 'Mum, do you think it was because I was always refusing to eat my Brussels sprouts?'

She held me tightly then, sobbing again.

Finally she said, 'Darling, that didn't have anything to do with it. This is simply something that happens, that can hit anyone at any time. You don't have to do anything to earn it, to make yourself deserve it.'

Then, tearfully, she told me how the one thing she wished most of all was that she could change places with me. What mother wouldn't?

The long evening dragged slowly by, a time of grief

and an immense sense of loneliness and terror. I thought endlessly of death, of dying, of not seeing out this life in full, of leaving behind everything and everyone I loved, of being denied the unfolding possibilities that I had started to glimpse ahead of me. Above all, around all, the same question endlessly hovered about me.

Why me?

Chapter 4

One evening, quite late, I was lying in my hospital bed, feeling grotty as usual, when I heard them ringing the bell in the corridor. Mum poked her head out to see what was going on.

'There's a surprise for you,' she said, when she came back in.

Anything was a welcome distraction from my endless hours of discomfort but even so, I was surprised when who should walk in but Father Christmas.

There he was in his red suit and white whiskers, carrying his big bag of parcels. He came over to my bed and let me pick out a couple of presents. They turned out to be a black pen and a little notepad. I was really touched and grateful to whoever it was who had gone to that trouble for me and all the other kids on the ward.

But afterwards my heart started sinking. Father Christmas had reminded me of the time of year, and the fact that I was going to have to spend Christmas here in this small room, surrounded by medical equipment, a long way from the rest of my family.

We're a close-knit family. I have two brothers and three sisters and we've always enjoyed each other's company. Even as the older ones had started growing up and leaving home they had stayed in the same area as Mum and Dad, so we remained close. Every year, no matter what, we all swarmed together again for the festive season.

I suddenly realized that this was going to be the first Christmas ever when we wouldn't all be with each other on Christmas Day and Boxing Day.

Mum must have seen and understood the expression on my face because, soon after Father Christmas had left us to continue on his rounds of the wards, she walked quietly out of my room.

I was left to my thoughts, which were not at all happy. I could hear Mum outside in the corridor, talking to my consultant and one of the nurses. I pricked up my ears, trying to listen to what they were saying. There was a long pause, then all three of them came back into the room. Mum was smiling.

'Katrina,' she said immediately. 'I've talked them into letting you go home for Christmas!'

'Really?' I said, completely bowled over by the news. 'When do we leave?'

'We'll give you one more looking-over,' said the consultant, who had followed her into the room. 'Then you can go home more or less straight away.'

I couldn't believe it. No news could have been more welcome.

An hour or so later I was in the car as we drove back

home to Milton Keynes. But now I was outside in the real world things no longer felt as good. For one thing the car journey, some forty miles or so, underlined to me just how far from home the hospital in Oxford really was. Also, I wasn't feeling any better for being out of hospital. I knew that simply being back at home would not make this Christmas the same as all the ones I was used to. I'd be confined to my bedroom, or at best I'd have to lie on the sofa and I wouldn't be able to get up and down. All I could think was that I'd make the best of it, try to enjoy myself as much as possible.

I was brought up in a large, happy family, with my two older brothers, Darren and Fenton, and two older sisters, Vanessa and Tanya. My little sister Janine is the baby of the family, taking over that role from me, coming along about ten years after me.

I knew my family always made the most of Christmas, and to me simply seeing them enjoy themselves would make me happy.

At last we were home, and after a little bit of quiet celebrating I went upstairs to bed. The funny thing is that of all years this was the first Christmas Eve when I wasn't so excited that I stayed awake half the night. I soon went to sleep.

It all brought back memories, because staying awake on Christmas Eve was one of those unofficial family traditions. Dad used to dress up as Father Christmas, just in case we were still awake or we actually woke up while he was around, and he would creep into our rooms to put out our presents. We used to wait for Father

Christmas to deliver our presents, pretending we were asleep, all sisters in the same bedroom, and when he had gone we used to sneak a look at a few of the presents.

We tried not to spoil the magic for the youngest, Janine. By now she was six and I had long since worked out the truth about Father Christmas. But Janine still believed in him.

There was one time when I was little, before Janine came along, when I was about nine or ten years old. Father Christmas came into the bedroom, all dressed up in robes and whiskers, and he obviously twigged that I was still awake. He didn't leave my presents there.

After he'd gone I went running down the stairs and I said to Mum, 'Father Christmas didn't bring me any presents!'

It was a terrible disaster!

She said, 'Well, it's obviously because you're still awake. I'll tell you what we can do: we'll put your Holly Hobby doll in your bed, make out it's you, and you're asleep. We'll hide in the bathroom, shall we? Maybe Father Christmas will come back and bring you presents after all.'

Of course I went into the bathroom and hid there with the light off. Shortly afterwards I heard this little sound and I said, 'That's Father Christmas's sleigh.'

And sure enough, when I went back to the bedroom, there was a sack of presents by my bed. I think it was the next day that the penny finally dropped and I worked out that perhaps it hadn't really been Father Christmas after all.

All that was a long time in the past, but in the inter-vening years we'd all kept a sort of pact, mainly for the benefit of Janine, and every Christmas Eve we would go through the same excited routine. Not this year, though. I was in bed early, my own bed, so comfortingly famil-iar, and I drifted off to sleep almost at once.

When I woke up in the morning I was greeted by a sight I could barely believe: a big sack of presents had appeared at the end of my bed. My sister's bed too. What was so incredible to me was that for the last month Mum had spent virtually every day and many nights with me at the hospital in Oxford. How and where did she find the time and energy to buy Christmas presents for six children?

Even now, years later, I still find it incredible to think of the trouble and expense she must have gone to, at a time when things were hard for the whole family.

Feeling after all that it really was Christmas, I got out of bed and my brother Fenton lugged my sackful of presents downstairs. We always did the same thing on Christmas Day: each of us picked our own places in the room, and settled in one chair. 'I'm in this chair today,' we'd say, fending each other off.

So I installed myself in my chosen chair but the first thing I saw when I sat down was the school photo Dad had collected. It was right next to my chair. And I looked at it and I saw me with my long blonde hair and I thought, 'My gosh, I can't believe I am going to lose my hair.'

I was getting emotional and tearful sitting there. I couldn't help it. I wanted, craved, to be normal, as I had assumed I had been only a few weeks earlier. Everything was the same as always, except that now I was completely different.

Mum spotted me getting upset.

She said, 'Come on darling, just open some of your presents.'

So I put on a brave face and began opening my first present. It came out and I looked at it in disbelief. It was a set of bendy rollers.

Mum had started buying our presents months before; with everything that had been going on she must have completely forgotten what she had bought and what had happened since.

I suppose I broke down. I can't see how I could not.

Mum must have felt terrible, because she kept cuddling and hugging me, saying how sorry she was, that she hadn't meant anything by it. I wanted to tell her, through my tears, that I understood, I really understood. I knew how these things happened: so much had been crammed into our lives recently, and she had six children and a husband to care for. I wasn't her only concern.

It all blew over in a few moments, and I put the rollers on the floor out of sight. Soon they were forgotten. We opened the rest of our presents and we all had a very nice, very easy Christmas morning.

Lunchtime came, but I was too ill to eat. No one drew any attention to it. That evening, though, I was lying on the settee and they said, 'Come on Katrina, you've got to get up, you've got to get up.'

By then I didn't have any more energy to get up. I said, 'No, I can't, I can't.'

But then one of them put on the song 'Love in the First Degree' by Bananarama. They knew it was mine and my sisters' song. Every year, birthday or Christmas, if that record comes on we're up on our feet straight away, we're dancing, and all our arms are up in the air.

That day, Bananarama came on and I went on just sitting there, feeling sorry for myself. I was thinking that I couldn't do it this time. It felt so unfair. But my sisters pulled me up from the settee and they held me, because by now I couldn't stand up unsupported any more. I was so weak, so ill.

They were doing the Bananarama song and I simply broke down. I couldn't help myself. The way I saw it was that this time last year we were doing the Bananarama song and I could do it perfectly, but now I could barely even stand without help.

I ended up outside in the hall, sitting on the bottom steps of the staircase. I rested my head in my hands, staring down at the carpet. Everyone else was still in the living room and I was briefly alone. I was thinking of my nans, because they had died. I was thinking to myself how sad it was to be without them, how they had always enjoyed our noisy, companionable Christmases, joining in with everything.

I was thinking: next year it could be me who's not here any more. When you've got grandparents, you know that each year they're getting older. You kiss them goodbye, and you think and hope without forming the words in your mind that they'll be there again next year.

But it's not only old age that can kill you, as I was discovering. Anyone can die, at any time. I was alone on those familiar stairs and I was crying about my nans, crying about my illness, and that's how that night ended for me.

Chapter 5

At Mum's suggestion I went to have my hair cut short before returning to hospital. I had now accepted the reality of what was going to happen to me, that there was no avoiding it.

It was a way of taking back control over a tiny part of my life. The whole idea of seeing my lovely long hair fall out, the hair I'd never cut in my life, was too awful to contemplate. Better, I believed, to take the initiative myself. It was terrible to see my long locks being snipped away, but at least it was the result of a decision, one I had taken myself.

When I was back in the Radcliffe Hospital in Oxford, the medical team came to my room with a prepared plan of what they were going to do to me. They explained in simple terms. They said they would begin with a short course of chemotherapy. I think the total they spoke of then was about five separate doses. These were supposed to shrink my tumour to a point where it would be safe to operate.

The initial treatment was starting now because the

sooner they acted, they said, the better. Delay could be dangerous. The tumour was still there inside me, still growing. There was an immediate danger of it spreading. They didn't use the word, but everything implied that they saw me as an emergency.

It was only at this point that I began to realize just how serious my situation was. Until then it had all been words alone: terrible, terrifying words, to be sure, but now we had moved into the realm of action.

Before they began the chemo treatment they told me, 'Katrina, this might make you feel nauseated. It will probably make you sick.'

That at least was clear, straightforward information, undisguised and candid. For once I knew what to expect.

It didn't take very long for the first dose to be administered, probably less than half an hour, but the precautions the team took were impressive and frightening. Clearly, the drugs were of maximum strength: no diluted version was given to me just because I was now officially a child. The chemo they gave me was in liquid form, injected directly into my veins. When the nursing staff walked into the room to start, they were all dressed in face masks and rubber gloves; presumably this was for their protection, not mine.

Not a long process in itself, but the consequences were to go on longer than I would have ever imagined possible. They began a couple of hours later. I suddenly started feeling extremely ill, nausea swimming through me. I sat up in bed and told Mum. She quickly brought across one of those little papier-mâché, hat-shaped bowls, and while she held me I threw up violently into it. I've always loathed being sick. When it started, I hated and dreaded the feeling more than anything else.

So there I was, suddenly more ill, and more spectacularly ill, than I had ever been in my life. The spasms came again and again, one after the other, a painful and unpleasant heaving and retching. I would recover slightly for a few minutes, think to myself that the worst must have passed, then it would return, more dramatically disagreeable than before. It lasted for hours until I was exhausted, wrung out, trembling with disgust and discomfort. My mum had been with me through it all, holding me, comforting me.

I felt a thought repeatedly forming in my mind. Is this worth it? I'm going to die soon, anyway. Why go through this when the outcome has been settled? How long is it going to go on?

Gradually, slowly, the feeling of sickness died down as the days went by. I still felt sick all the time, but at least I wasn't constantly throwing up. Of much more immediate discomfort was the fact that in the second week I was in hospital I began developing really nasty ulcers inside my mouth. Eating became painful, just at the time when, with the receding need to vomit, I had begun to feel like taking food again.

I ate and drank barely anything during the first week; in the second week I managed to get down only a tiny bit more. I was constipated and dehydrated, in awful discomfort. They kept giving me saline to help, but nothing really helps you when you're undergoing chemotherapy.

Part of the problem was to do with my age. Being sixteen I was, in terms of cancer treatment, on the cusp between childhood and adulthood. I was suffering from a childhood tumour, though, and as a result was being treated with chemotherapy designed for children. Unlike other medicines – e.g. junior aspirin – childhood chemo is not a diluted version of the adult treatment. It is a different kind, with as many radical and unpleasant effects on the body as the adult medication. As a rule, the older the child the more traumatic the side-effects. As a sixteen-year-old 'child' I was experiencing the full blast of unpleasant reactions to these extremely strong medicines.

I was allowed home briefly before the second course began, another welcome break from hospital, in spite of the fact that I continued to feel wretched. Making things even worse this time was signs of my hair starting to fall out. I would find several strands on my pillow in the mornings, and combing or brushing it was something I was doing with great gentleness.

One evening I was upstairs having a bath and washing my hair not really thinking about what I was doing. Then, as I was rinsing it, I realized a lot of hair was coming out into my hands. I couldn't help it – I began crying.

Janine, my little sister, still only six years old, must have heard me because she came running in.

'What's the matter, Katrina?' she said.

'It's all right, Janine,' I said. 'Don't worry about it.'

'No. I want to help.'

I couldn't think what to say to her. Then, on her own, she noticed that the bath water had a lot of my hair floating around.

She said, 'Don't worry, don't worry! Look, look at this.' She took a face-flannel, rinsed it out, and held it out to me. 'Put this over your eyes.'

I pressed it against my face, thinking it might be a game.

'What are you doing?' I said.

While I couldn't see she took a few squares from the toilet roll, then used them to scoop the hair up from the bath and put it into the toilet. I began peeping out from behind the face flannel, trying to see what she was doing, and she said, 'Don't look, don't look. You can't look yet.'

When she had found every single hair in the bath, put it down the toilet and flushed the lot away, she said, 'I'll rinse your hair now.'

I'll never forget that simple act of sisterly friendship. Ever since then I've thought of her as my real soulmate. In those few moments she became someone I would care for and protect more than anybody or anything else in the world.

After that short respite at home I returned to hospital and the second course of chemotherapy began.

I can only say this simply: it was worse than the first time.

Not long after the second course started, I became

really ill. I weathered the worst of it for about one month, but then my mum asked the hospital if there would be any chance I could go home for a couple of days. I was aching to be out of that confining little room, and back in familiar surroundings once more, if only for a short time.

But one of the problems with a course of chemotherapy is that your immune system suffers a great knocking about. In hospital I was being kept in as clean and antiseptic an environment as possible. Doors and windows were kept closed, and much of what went in and out of the room had to be passed through a little shutter window. No one could enter unless they were wearing gloves and a mask. The medical staff were also choosy about who they would let into the room to visit me.

The request to let me home for a while was conditional on my blood-count picking up, so for the next few days I watched the results of these tests with some anxiety. In the end, to my great relief, the count did start improving slightly so Mum and I immediately repeated our request. This time it was granted.

It was a break for both of us, and it allowed Mum to go back to work for a few days. Considering she had been working for John Lewis for only a comparatively short time, they had been fantastically supportive of her, and generous with letting her take time away. So far my illness had run for about two months, and Mum had been with me for most of that time.

I found my brother Fenton at home, and when he had

44

worked out the situation he said straight away, 'Look, Mum, if you want to get back to work, I can stay here with Katrina and look after her.'

We're all the same in our family. Fenton knew that Mum didn't like taking too much time off work, any more than I did then or have ever done since.

Also, behind her eagerness to get back to work was, I'm sure, a pretty clear realization that I was far from finished with the worst of my illness, and that later in the year she would be needing to spend even more time with me.

So for a while my brother Fenton looked after me at home. I'd known Fenton all my life, of course, but he'd always given out this image of not being an emotional man, that he wasn't someone who cared. We'd always been close and we'd always been friends, but we had never really opened up to each other before.

During this period, while he was nursing me at home, we began a slow process of learning about each other's deeper sides. The process was only just beginning, and I think neither of us at that stage would have admitted it was going on, when another crisis suddenly struck.

I was experiencing a great deal of pain, perhaps the worst agony I'd known since my illness had begun.

'I can't deal with this on my own, Katrina,' he said in the end.

'Then ring Mum at work,' I said, pleading with him. 'She'll know what to do.'

I think he was only too relieved to have that decision taken out of his hands.

First he phoned Mum, then somehow he managed to get me into his car and we drove over to John Lewis's to collect her. We went straight down to Casualty at Milton Keynes Hospital, and from there I was taken to the children's ward. The nursing sister, who remembered me from my last visit, was obviously shocked to see what I looked like. By this time I had gone completely yellow; even the whites of my eyes were yellow!

The sister said to my mum, 'Look, there's no time. We're going to send her straight over to the John Radcliffe.'

An ambulance arrived, I was bundled in, and we set off across the countryside towards Oxford at high speed. I was feeling too ill to take much notice, but I was a little disappointed that they didn't sound the siren.

An odd feature of this short, hectic journey was that as well as Mum being in the back of the ambulance with me, the nursing sister had come along too. What she didn't know at the time (although she was soon to find out) was that she was several weeks pregnant. So there was I, strapped to the bunk in the ambulance, as ill as I had ever been in my life, and there too was the nurse who was throwing up half the time! Inevitably, the poor woman's plight only made me feel worse.

We finally reached the Radcliffe, and I was rushed to an emergency room. They quickly examined me, and soon came to the grave diagnosis of what had happened. Clearly I was suffering from jaundice, but what they wanted to know was why. What was causing the jaundice?

It didn't take them long to work it out. My tumour was reacting to the chemotherapy, and now it had burst.

'We're going to have to carry out an emergency operation,' they explained.

Obviously they had not been expecting the tumour to burst. What they had repeatedly told me, and I knew they meant it, was that the course of chemotherapy was intended to shrink the tumour. Clearly, the fact that it had suddenly burst was as much of a shock to them as it was to me.

At first I thought, 'Maybe it doesn't matter. Maybe it's like a boil bursting. A bit unpleasant, but it will relieve the pressure and all the bad stuff can flow out.'

But I heard them discussing it amongst themselves, and I quickly picked up what most concerned them. They knew that if the tumour had burst, then bits of it could spread around my body, get into my bloodstream. Once that happened, then it could start reproducing itself anywhere inside my body.

Despair welled up inside me again. All I kept hearing were the words 'emergency' and 'operation', and I had this terrible pain inside me, I was losing my hair, I was losing weight, I was sick all the time. I asked myself, again and again, can any of this really be worth it? I was convinced by then that I was going to die, no matter what. Couldn't they just leave me alone to die peacefully, without these emergencies, all this drastic treatment?

Mum saw me, and she asked me what I was thinking.

Crying, I told her. 'It's not worth it, Mum. Tell them to let me go.'

She held my hand, and pressed herself close to me.

All she said was, 'No, you're not going to die, Katrina.'

'I am,' I insisted.

'You're not. You just hold on, let these people do what they do best. And you're doing what you do best. You've beaten the worst of it. Just keep trying, darling.'

I can't remember a time when Mum wasn't praising me, and not just after I became ill. She was the same with all her children. Big things and little, she was always there to praise us, give us confidence. Sometimes the little things were silly, but it always helped. Once, during one of the times when I wasn't eating well, I remember sitting there with most of my dinner still in front of me. I couldn't face any more, and was pushing the rest of it around the plate.

Mum said, 'Katrina, you've got to eat, you must keep up your strength.'

'I don't want any more.'

'You've hardly eaten anything. Look, what about the potatoes? You love roast potatoes.'

'Not these.'

'Go on, eat one more.'

'No, Mum.'

And she'd say, 'You've done really well. Why don't you finish off one more potato?'

And so I would, and maybe even a little more of the rest of the food. A bit of encouragement and praise, it does help you tremendously. She knew, and I was learning, that so long as hope remained alive, so long as my spirit burned high, I had a chance of beating this disease.

Making me finish that potato was her way of saying, 'You're going to get through this, Katrina.'

Now, years after this first attack of the cancer, she has confessed to me that in those early days of my illness she sometimes doubted I would get through it, but I never caught so much as a glimpse of that. Never, at any time, did she glow with less than complete confidence in me, total belief in my ability to rise above the disease.

I know it saved me.

But there was still the emergency of the burst tumour to get through.

They said to me, 'Look Katrina, after the operation we'll be keeping you under observation.'

'What does that mean?' I asked, knowing by now that when they went out of their way to tell me or warn me, they had something up their sleeves.

'Well, it means that we'll be taking you to the Intensive Care Unit. We don't want to alarm you. We'd like to take you down there now, before the operation, so you can have a look round.'

'Why should I want to do that?'

'It would help you. You can see what goes on down there, so that when you're in Intensive Care there won't seem to be so many mysteries about what's going on.'

They explained that the operation I was about to have was a serious one, and in the aftermath I'd need a lot of nursing.

'The main difference between Intensive Care and a

normal recovery ward is that we have people there twenty-four hours a day, and there's a lot of equipment on hand. It helps us keep an eye on you, and prevent things going wrong before we know they've started.'

'But I always thought Intensive Care was where people were taken who . . .'

'These days it's part of our normal routine. Some patients go into recovery wards, and others go into Intensive Care. Why don't you come and have a look round?'

So I went down there, and they were almost right. My mental image of the place, based on TV programmes, was of terrible events taking place on the point of death. In reality, the Intensive Care Unit was just another area of the hospital, where a lot of well-trained and highly professional nurses went about their work with great efficiency. There was a huge amount of electronic monitoring equipment being used. This was undeniably impressive. On the other hand, most of the patients already in there did look extremely ill.

I looked at them and I thought, 'Oh my God! Is it coming to this?'

For the first time I really began to wonder if anyone except my mum believed I was going to come through.

They told me I was going to have the operation the next day. Back in my room they started the early tests and preparations, and then I was left alone with Mum, Dad and my little sister Janine.

I knew that what was about to happen was the big event, the major operation. I was nervous and I was feeling upset. A conviction grew in me that I wasn't going to come through this, but even so I simply wanted it to be over and done with.

We were forty miles from home, and Dad had to leave with Janine. She kissed me goodbye as she was leaving and all I could think was, 'I'm never going to see you again!'

I held her tightly, not wanting to let go. I honestly thought I'd never see her again. She was only six, but somehow I had a feeling that she was thinking the same thing about me.

Then Dad kissed me goodnight. Saying goodbye to them that night was the hardest thing I've ever had to do in my life, because I really believed I was saying goodbye to them for ever.

I slept fitfully, even though I was exhausted by all the things that were happening.

In the morning I had my pre-med, and whenever I was alone with Mum I kept saying to her, 'Do I have to have it? Do I have to have this operation, Mum?'

She said, 'Look at the agony you are in. They're going to make you better.'

'Wouldn't it just be better to let me go?' I said. 'I could have some quality time, quality life. I'd be at home, I'd be with you and Dad and the others. I'd be in my own life, not here.'

'No, you've got to get better, darling.'

'But I'm not going to come through this operation, am I?'

She said, 'You will come through, I know it.'

'I'm not going to, Mum.'

'Don't say that, Katrina. These people know what they're doing. They're the best in the world. This hospital is famous all over the country. And this time they've got you. All you have to do is hold on, believe in yourself.'

The staff were now all around me, and soon they came to take me down to the theatre. I was feeling woozy from the pre-med, but Mum was there and Dad had driven down to be with me.

A man in a surgical mask tried to make me smile, then he took my left wrist in his hand. I felt pressure on my arm and a slight tingle as the needle was pressed into me.

He said, 'I want you to count to ten, Katrina. I'll bet you can't get past five.'

I think I got as far as four.

Chapter 6

A long day passed, and I knew nothing of it.

The next thing I remember, it was really late the same day. The operation had begun in the morning, but I did not recover consciousness until late in the evening. When I woke up I saw my Auntie Gill there, and my mum's face looking anxiously at me. As soon as I could take stock I realized that I had been placed close to the nurses' station. My first thought was, 'I'm not in Intensive Care!'

The relief from that was immense.

I mean, I had tubes coming out from almost every part of my body, but what really mattered to me was that I wasn't in Intensive Care. I said this to Mum.

She said, 'No darling.'

I woke up feeling as if I had been in a long, peaceful sleep. The reality, of course, was that it was a drug-induced state, and the anaesthetic was only slowly wearing off. But the effect was much the same. I felt peaceful and rested.

I was drifting in and out of consciousness all through

that night, and gradually returned to something resembling normality. They kept me by the nurses' station for a few more days because they wanted to keep an eye on me. This was a sort of halfway stage, between being in a general ward and in Intensive Care.

One of my first and most urgent needs, that night of the operation, was something to drink. I asked for some water.

'I'm sorry,' said the duty nurse. 'You're not allowed anything at all to eat or drink.'

'Just a sip,' I said, wondering if I had to plead.

'We can't give you anything. I'm ever so sorry.'

I began mouthing, 'Water, water, water . . .' like a character in a desert film, and in the end they took pity on me.

They gave me a little pink stick, like a lolly stick with a little sponge on the end. They put this in some cold water and let me suck on the sponge.

The first thing I discovered was that I wasn't strong enough to hold even that! So Mum or Janine would put the stick to my mouth and I'd suck on it like a baby.

The need for water became my major craving. My body temperature was constantly shifting up and down, and sometimes I felt really hot and uncomfortable. At times like this I was desperate for some water.

My mum came in one day with some lolly sticks, and she used to put these in an ice tray in the freezer and let me suck on the cubes. The nurses let me do this, always provided I wasn't taking in too much of the water.

I would say to Mum, 'Oh Mum, I'd love an ice-cube.'

She would reply, 'I'm sorry, darling, they're not ready yet. You're going to have to wait a while.'

Those times waiting for the ice were some of the longest hours of my life.

Finally they moved me away from the nurses' station and put me back in my own little room once more. I knew then that I must be getting a bit better.

The next trouble was looming: they wanted me up on my feet as soon as possible. After major surgery you have to keep your blood circulation going, otherwise you get blood clots in your legs.

The physiotherapist would say, 'You really must try, Katrina. Come out and walk.'

The problem was that at this point I had a catheter going into my bladder, there were about four tubes coming out of my left side and three more coming out of my right, with more in both my arms. I had another tube coming out of my nose and they wanted me out of bed and moving my legs.

I could not stand the catheter between my legs. I just didn't want it there.

The physio was lifting up my leg and I said, 'Ouch, you're touching my catheter.'

'You've got to move, Katrina!'

'Oh no, I can't do that – my catheter's moving,' I said, just wanting them to stop.

So in the end one of the physios held my catheter in so it wouldn't move, while the other moved my legs up and down. In the end it began to work, and then it felt like a real achievement. As the days went on a few tubes were removed – the relief that brought!

I wasn't too concerned about blood clots forming in my legs – what I wanted was to get rid of the tubes. Each one that went was like winning a prize. The one I most wanted gone was the catheter. I didn't much care for my nose one either – if I sat up in bed it would dangle like an elephant's trunk.

Once, I said to Mum, 'Will you promise me one thing? Whatever else lies ahead, I won't ever have to have a tube go down my throat or up my nose?'

'I promise you,' she said. 'If that's what you don't want, I will never let you have that done. I promise you that.'

Through all this I was undergoing sedation by morphine, so I wasn't in too much pain. In fact I was on a high! Morphine did nothing for discomfort, though, so the unpleasant feelings brought on by all the tubes remained a bit of a preoccupation. But, as I say, one by one the tubes were coming out so life was definitely improving.

Late one night, Mum said to me, 'You know, Katrina, you really must try to get out of bed. They want to get you out of bed now.'

It was about a week after the operation.

'It's too soon,' I said.

'No, I've been listening to what they say,' Mum replied. 'You've got to make an effort. This business of the blood clots in your legs isn't a joke. If one of those forms, it could be serious.'

The next day they started to take me off the

morphine. It was beginning to have an adverse effect on me: I would sit up in bed and stare off into the distance.

Mum would say to me, 'Katrina, what are you staring at?'

'What?' I would say, snappily. 'What are you going on about?'

She would glance over her shoulder, in the direction I was looking.

Then, 'What *are* you staring at?'

At this time I was in room with a lot of glass panels in the walls, giving the impression there was much to see outside. When I started the staring, apparently my eyes would poke out and it would seem that I was really staring at something. It always made Mum uneasy; she kept looking over her shoulder, or following my gaze, and there was never anything there.

The drugs were changing me into someone with a completely different personality. Mum knew I would never have done this before I became ill. It was a side-effect of the morphine, and obviously the medical staff knew that it could do weird things to their patients. It got so bad that one day Mum called a doctor in and asked him what was going on.

He examined me briefly, then said, 'Mrs Leeder, have you ever seen a drug addict before?'

'Not that I know,' she replied. 'No.'

'Well, I'm afraid you're looking at one now.'

He explained that morphine is what heroin comes from, and so the constituents that make heroin an addictive drug are fully present in morphine. He said that it was common practice in hospitals to treat major pain with substantial and repeated doses of morphine, but that as soon as possible they would start reducing the doses on a daily basis. The patients had to be weaned away from it. This was the process I was going through.

It was a real high to be on morphine. There was a little tube through which it was fed into me: I'd watch it gradually running down, slowly running out of the morphine. It was like a wind-up clock – going down and down we go, down we go.

I didn't care what it did to me. All I knew was that I was drifting slowly, seeing as I never had before, only faintly aware of the real world around me. That was the idea, wasn't it? The real world for me was the aftermath of a massive operation, a traumatic operation to remove an immense tumour, one so large it had burst under its own pressure. I couldn't cope with that physically: the pain would be too great. Better, surely, to drift unknowingly? But that is obviously why they have to wean their patients away from the morphine.

All through this period of my treatment Mum was writing up my diary for me. When I saw what she was doing I said, 'I want to try and write now.'

It came as a shock to discover that I couldn't write! No matter how I tried, I simply could not write. My little sister who was only six could write better than me.

I said to Mum, 'You know, I can't believe this. I'm a born-again baby, aren't I?'

And for that, it had taken nearly a week or so before I could talk again, until I could make myself understood. I wasn't even eating solids. I was on mashed-up liquidized foods – I was being fed, Mum was feeding me. I disliked everything about this. It was not *me*! I wasn't doing anything for myself. I couldn't eat without help, I couldn't even write in my own diary.

I was grumbling to Mum about this one day, so frustrated was I. At one point she went out of the room to get me a drink. Lying there alone, I thought, 'I'm going to surprise her!'

When no one was looking, I wriggled gently and slowly until I was on the edge of the bed, got my legs around to the side, and then I was upright. I walked slowly as far as the nurses' station. It was the first time I'd walked properly since the operation, and I'd done it on my own!

Mum came back with the drink and saw me standing there, all alone and holding on to my drip stands. She couldn't believe it was me. Some of the nurses came by and we all laughed a little, and talked excitedly, then with my mum's help I walked back slowly to my room.

One day Christine, the play teacher, gave me a big notepad and some felt-tipped pens. She said, 'Right, Katrina, try and draw.'

It was so difficult. I could *see* and *feel* the pen in my hand; I could stare at the white paper sheet in front of me. But connecting the two, drawing a familiar shape or line. That was beyond me. Christine came to my room every day and taught me things. But it was so difficult.

On top of everything else, I was back on the chemotherapy.

The day after my operation, while I was still groping my way back to consciousness, coming to terms with all the drips and tubes and catheters, they told me that although the operation had been a success they were going to put me on chemo straight away.

The aftermath of all those hours of surgery, plus the impact of the morphine, would have been enough for anyone. On top of that they wanted to inflict more chemo on me. This was going to be my third course. What else could I do but let it begin?

Chapter 7

Soon after the third round of chemo began I started to feel a tingling sensation in my feet and fingers. The next time I saw the consultant I told him about it. He did not seem too concerned. He reminded me of the problem of being a sixteen-year-old having the childhood chemo drugs given to me.

'The tingling is a side-effect of those,' he said helpfully. 'It's a drug called vincristine that causes temporary numbness. It's a powerful drug, and in fact it's the one that has caused your hair to fall out.'

I told him I was really worried about my feet.

He seemed to dismiss it. 'Don't worry. It's only temporary. It will wear off. Try rubbing them if it gets any worse.'

Well, it did not wear off. It got worse and rubbing them was pointless.

Once again I found myself saying to my mother, 'Mum, I've had enough. I have had *enough*!'

'Katrina, don't be silly,' she replied. 'Look, you're nearly through it now. We've come so far.'

'Is this the last course of chemo?'

She frowned for a moment, then said, 'Mmm . . . no darling, no. There's going to be a bit more than that.'

'Another week?'

She said, 'I'm afraid it's more than that. It's so hard to tell you this, but I think I heard them say it might be another year.'

I was stunned by this news.

'What do you mean, another *year* of chemotherapy? They told me the operation was a success!'

'It was, darling. In every way. But you have to have chemotherapy just in case any of the cancer cells had moved away from your kidney before they operated. If they did, they might still be distributed in your body. The chemotherapy will kill any cancer cells that might be around.'

It was another low-point. I had been bracing myself for another week of this hell, maybe another two weeks. But a whole year!

It stretched off endlessly into the imaginable future, dominating everything. A year of pain, vomiting, ulcerated mouth, numb limbs. It was all too much to bear. Even thinking about it was too much. Life lost its purpose.

At that point there was no light at the end of the tunnel, because the tunnel was too long.

I had a couple of bad days, deep in depression and grief.

Mum was sleeping in the room with me. She had started out by trying to doze uncomfortably in a chair, sitting upright, wrapped in a sleeping bag. After a few days one of the nurses, realizing that Mum wasn't going to go away until I was better, a lot better, found her a spare mattress and laid it on the floor for her. After that, Mum was a little more comfortable, but it couldn't have been pleasant for her.

We had our own television and video in the room with us, and a little bathroom just outside the door. After a week or so it started to feel a bit like a home from home. The nurses too did what they could to make it more homely. They realized I was in for a long stint.

With the onset of the third course of full chemo, my body no longer functioned as it should for normal things. I couldn't go to the toilet properly, I couldn't walk, I still couldn't talk properly, and I couldn't use my hands.

Christine, the play lady, was working on the pain and disability in my extremities. She came in most days with some small task for me to take on, anything that would exercise my hands. For instance, one day she had me trying to make badges with my fingers.

But it was my feet that were the serious problem. The sensation of tingling quickly got worse, and became a stabbing pain. If you can imagine the worst case of pins and needles you've ever had, then add to that someone gripping your foot as tightly as possible, while repeatedly stabbing at it with a sharp knife, you will get some idea of what it was like. It was excruciating.

They said I had to exercise my feet, to try and walk on them. This would probably make the sensation die down. In reality, the moment I put pressure on my feet the pain was much worse.

The only way I could get around was to walk on tiptoes. Anyway, I couldn't walk at all unless I had someone to hold on to. I had my intravenous machine – the device with the saline drip – so I would hold on to that.

What a sight I must have been – drugged to the eyeballs, bald as a billiard ball, limping along on tiptoes and clutching a drip-holder.

I was forever being told, 'Katrina, please – you must try and walk on the whole of your feet, on the balls of your feet. You can't keep walking around on tiptoes.'

Soon after this I was given another big dose of chemotherapy, with the result that I suffered really bad diarrhoea. I was on two drips at the time so I had two big blue boxes full of drips going through, one in each arm. I also had a tube going into a major blood vessel in my chest, close to my heart.

And then, troubles piling on troubles, I found out something else from a chance remark from a stranger. It seemed there was no end to this!

The background to it was that the medical staff had, without saying anything to me, advised Mum and Dad that I should take advice from a psychiatrist. Their point apparently was that some patients are severely traumatized when they realize the extent of the surgery they have been through.

Mum had said straight away, 'I'm sorry but my daughter is not going to need a psychiatrist.'

'I think it would help Katrina to talk to one,' said the consultant, not giving up on a mother's say-so.

Mum apparently replied, 'Well, I don't, but we'll ask Katrina.'

The first I knew of this was when my parents told me about the conversation, and asked me what I thought.

Straight away I said, 'I don't want a psychiatrist.'

Shortly after this, we heard the dinner lady in the hall and Mum went out of the room to collect my dinner. While she was gone the door suddenly burst open and a woman I'd never seen before came charging in. I noticed she wasn't wearing a mask or gloves.

'Excuse me,' I said. 'You're not supposed to . . .'

She interrupted me without apology.

'I don't have time to talk at the moment. I was just letting you know that because you haven't got your kidney now . . .'

'What do you mean?' I said. 'What do you mean that I don't have a kidney?'

Her entire manner, and intrusive way of speaking to me, was seriously rubbing me up the wrong way.

'You ought to know you lost your kidney in the operation,' she said.

'I don't know what you're going on about!' I said, but my head was beginning to spin with this new and unwelcome information.

At that moment Mum came back into the room and said, 'Excuse me, who are you?'

The woman gave her name, and added that she was a consultant psychiatrist.

'I don't care who you are,' Mum said stoutly. 'You can't just barge in here without an appointment.'

'I don't think you understand . . .'

I was crying by now. Mum glanced at me in desperation.

'It's you who doesn't understand,' she said to the woman. 'Please leave straight away.'

To her credit the woman did leave then.

As soon as we were alone together, Mum said, 'Why are you crying, Katrina? What has she said to you?'

'She told me I haven't got a kidney,' I said, between sobs. 'Is that true, Mum? Did they remove one of my kidneys?'

'Oh darling, I'm so sorry,' said Mum. 'Where is that bloody woman?'

She went out and hurried away down the corridor. From the satisfied expression on her face when she returned a few minutes later, I gathered she had found her and given her a piece of her mind.

But the damage had been done by then.

I was thinking, 'Why didn't I know? Why didn't anyone tell me anything?'

It seemed to me that yet again I was being protected to the point where everyone but me knew what was going on. But it was my body, *my* life! As well as I could I said this to Mum.

She said, 'But Katrina, would you honestly have wanted to know? If we'd told you before you went down for your op, what would you have thought?'

I would have thought: this is my body, my life.

But would I?

After a moment I said, 'Well, I would have thought that it meant I was definitely going to die.'

'Exactly,' said Mum. 'Now do you see that we were only trying to protect you?'

'Yes, but . . .'

'It wouldn't have done you any good to know before the operation. And we were planning to tell you as soon as you were feeling stronger.'

'But, Mum.'

'I didn't realize that interfering woman was going to come in and say something to you.'

I knew Mum was probably right. I couldn't face not knowing these things, but even less could I face knowing them. Even so, in my miserable state, more ill and uncomfortable than I had ever been in my life, drugged and weak, I had to face up to the fact that I had lost one of my kidneys. Once again, death nudged against me.

I hope no other parent has to decide whether to hold back or reveal such terrible pieces of information to their children.

One of the doses of chemo gave me a really bad attack of diarrhoea. It was disgusting, painful and humiliating. All through the night I had to keep waking my mum and asking her to help me, because I had to use a commode. I couldn't bend down low enough to use the toilet because my scar hurt so much, but I couldn't use the commode unassisted because it had a lid, and I didn't even have enough strength to lift that.

All through that night, at about half-hourly intervals,

I had to keep waking up my mum. I could see that, even though she was trying not to show it, she was really exhausted. I would hold on as long as possible, until things got desperate, then as gently as possible I would say, 'Mum . . . I'm sorry, Mum, but I've got to go again.'

With the expression on her face revealing her fatigue she would help me out of bed; I couldn't even do that without her. Then she would practically lift me on to the commode and sit with me until I'd finished. She had to sleep in my room too, and no one wants a messy potty when they're trying to sleep, so her next chore was always to take the thing away to empty it.

This happened six or seven times during the night, and on that seventh time I remember her saying, 'Oh God.'

All I could say was, 'I'm so sorry, Mum.'

'Oh no, darling! I'm the sorry one! I'm really sorry. I didn't mean to say that. I don't mind how many times you have to go.'

She kept saying this. But whenever she went back to her mattress on the floor she was asleep in moments. I knew she was exhausted.

Then I had to go again!

I decided to try to make it on my own. Next to my bed there were two large stands which held my bags of drips. One of these held the line which ran directly into a vein close to my heart. Now the nurses had said to me and Mum many times, 'If ever you get an air bubble in one of these lines, you're to let us know straight away. If a large amount of air gets into your heart you can die.'

I levered myself up in the bed and held on to one of the stands. Mum was flat out on her mattress, already in deep sleep. She didn't wake. I managed to get upright, then stand on my own, leaning against the stand. I set off slowly across the room, one tiny step at a time, pushing the stand in front of me. The commode was not all that far away.

Then one of the stand wheels caught itself in Mum's quilt. I completely lost my balance. The stand toppled over, I crashed down on top of Mum, and immediately the alarm on the machine went off. Before the nurse arrived, Mum woke up.

'What the. . . ?' she said in her confusion.

'I'm sorry,' I said at once. 'I had to get to the toilet again.'

She was struggling to get up, but she had me, the stand and a tangle of tubes all over her.

Then the nurse arrived and immediately sorted everything out.

Afterwards, when order had been restored, and I'd used the commode again, Mum and I were both wide awake.

Mum said, 'On no account must you do that again. I'm here to help you, darling. You can wake me up a hundred times a night and I won't mind. You must always wake me up if you need me.'

Chapter 8

One day I had just been given a new round of chemotherapy and I was so ill that all I could do was lie on my bed and cry. There were many times like that, when there was nothing left in the world to do but feel miserable. I was told it was natural and normal to cry after these things, but sometimes I felt so terribly sad, so miserable and *finished* that I couldn't believe it was in any way normal.

On this day I was really crying and Mum was in the room.

She sat there silently for a while, but then she said, 'Come on, Katrina, you don't need to cry alone. Let's cry together.'

It happened spontaneously like that. The next minute we were side by side on the bed, bawling our eyes out. It helped to have Mum there, but it made the crying worse. It has that effect, if someone shows you love when you're miserable.

When I could find the breath to speak, I said to Mum,

'Look, I really feel this is the end of my life. I can't ever see it getting better. They give me chemotherapy, and I'm sick for a week, I'm sick for a whole week. Before I get over that they give me even more. I get ulcers in my mouth, I can't eat, I can't drink, I can't move, I can't do *anything*!'

While I was talking I was moving around in my distress, and one of the tubes, taped against my arm, close to the stitches around the incision, was pulled slightly. It was the chemo line that ran into my chest, close to my heart.

Mum noticed that more of it was looping free, and she said, 'What's happened there?'

I pulled at it, and a little more came out. I thought I could end all the chemo, there and then, if I could get the thing out of my chest.

I got my free hand up to it, and Mum said, 'What are you doing?'

'I'm going to finish it now!' I cried.

She grabbed my arm desperately to stop me pulling the line further out.

'I've had enough!' I sobbed. 'I want to end the treatment now! I've had enough!'

Mum kept hold of my arm, pushing me down on the bed. But I was determined, and with all the strength I had, I began trying to get my fingers into the loop to just snatch the thing out. I could see that several stitches had opened, and I managed to pull the tube a little more.

Mum was shouting to the nurses for help.

Thankfully, as it turned out, there was a bit of spare

length on this tube, to compensate for accidental pulling. So in fact I did no serious harm to myself, but I had managed to pull it out a short distance and some of the stitches were ripped in the process.

All this became clear when the nurses came to Mum's assistance and got me under control. Soon they had me stretched out on a treatment bed, and sewed me up again. I was still struggling and sobbing, but they had me under restraint and there was little I could do.

I kept saying, 'I want to end the chemo. This is no good. I want to end it.'

But the nurses were businesslike and efficient and they simply took no notice of me, holding me down and repairing the damage to the incision and the tube. They did all this without an anaesthetic; I realize now they were probably teaching me a small lesson.

It was also at this stage that I knew the last of my hair was falling out. Mum kept saying to me, 'You look gorgeous Katrina. You look really pretty.'

I couldn't believe she meant that.

'Mum, I know I don't,' I said. 'I've never felt so terrible in my life.'

But she kept on at me.

'I want to take some photographs of you,' she said.

'That's the last thing I want.'

'You'll be glad one day.'

'Oh no, no, *no*! I don't want photographs of me like this.'

She said, 'Look, you'll thank me, I promise you. I'll take some photographs of you and I promise you that, with time, you'll look at them and you'll think, "Look how far I've come since those days." '

All I could say was, 'No I won't, Mum.'

But she got me to sit in my wheelchair and took her camera out.

'Come on, come on,' she said. 'You must smile!'

I found a smile from somewhere, a faked smile. I couldn't have felt less like smiling.

Mum snapped a few shots, and kept saying to me, 'It's for the best. In the future, you're going to look back at today, and . . .' I turned on my best and most insincere smile. 'Oh, that's wonderful. You look beautiful, you look really beautiful.' Actually, when I look back I'm so glad Mum took these photos. They show just how far I've progressed.

I couldn't even look at myself in the mirror at this time. There was a mirror in the room, but I would not look at it. Mum kept urging me to see myself, and I kept refusing.

She would say, 'Come on, Katrina, let's make today the day you look at yourself. I'll be right behind you.'

'No Mum, I can't today, not today.'

'Are you sure?'

'I'm terrified of what I'll see.'

'I know you are, darling. But this is part of getting better. Already you look a hundred times better than you did after the operation. Every day you look more beautiful. I want you to see that too, and see yourself getting better.'

She kept on at me. One day she went out to collect my

dinner, and I had a few moments on my own. I thought, 'I think I will have a little look after all.'

I staggered out of bed, and hobbled across to the wall where the mirror was. Always until now I had deliberately looked away. This time, bracing myself, I stared directly in.

I saw someone who looked like ET. It was one of the most shocking moments of my life. My face was a triangle of bones and sharp corners, my neck was string and bones, my cheeks had sunk in, my chin was a point, my eyes were like great balls hanging in deep, dark sockets. I had little wisps of hair, fragments of hair, clinging to tiny parts of my shining, naked skull.

By the time Mum returned to my room I was crying yet again. It was plain to me that recovery from cancer meant undergoing a long sequence of shocks and reverses.

For a long time nothing seemed to improve. After I'd been in hospital for a total of about three months I reached a stage where I was unable to eat a thing. It wasn't just a question of not being able to face food – which was true enough – but if I did manage to force something down I'd bring it up again soon afterwards. I'd gone down to weighing under six stone.

They put me on yet another drip. This one was a protein supplement, in effect two different kinds of food. They cost something between a hundred and a hundred and fifty pounds a time. I would be given them about three times a day.

The nurses would say, 'Look, Katrina, we don't care

what you eat. Anything you like would be OK. Six chocolate eclairs or five Mars bars. The only thing that matters is that you should put on some weight. Unless you do, the chemotherapy is going to win. It will get the better of you.'

I did what I could, but unless you've been through chemo you can never understand how impossible some things become.

During this long period I felt isolated from all my school friends. Very few of them came to visit me; most of my visitors were family. To a certain extent I do understand: the hospital was miles from home.

But it drew me closer to my family in ways I would never have anticipated.

Take my brother Fenton, for instance. Out of the six of us, if there's one who could be described as 'hard' it would be Fenton. He's not an emotional man. He always portrays himself as being very strong and I can't remember a time when he ever kissed or cuddled me. On the whole we were a close, affectionate family, but there was not much affection between me and Fenton. Yes, he would be there for everyday things. If I needed to be picked up from school, for instance, he would be waiting at those school gates for me. But he had never been one to show love, or give you a cuddle.

One day, though, Fenton came up to see me in my hospital room. It was actually the day on which I'd looked at myself in the mirror, so I was at my lowest. He hadn't seen me for about a week and I knew I'd lost more weight in that time. I think Fenton took this to mean that I'd deteriorated even more.

He came into the room and I sensed at once that he wanted to hold me. He said, 'Katrina, I want to give you a cuddle but I'm frightened you might break.'

I was so thin, my morale was at its lowest. I was amazed by his words, but only too happy that he wanted to cuddle me.

He held me warmly in his arms and gave me a kiss and he cuddled me and he said, 'I really love you, Katrina.'

With that he ran out of the room.

Mum followed him out and I could hear him in the corridor. He was sobbing, and he was banging the wall with his fists.

'Why has it happened to her?' he said loudly and miserably. 'It should have happened to me! I can't understand it, Mum.'

'Katrina's doing fine, Fenton,' I heard Mum say.

'Is she going to live?'

I had never heard him cry so much before. After a few minutes he came back into the room, red-eyed and look-ing bashful. He came straight to my bed and gave me another huge cuddle.

From that day Fenton has never hidden his feelings from anyone. I think that's done him the world of good as well, to let something like that come out.

This day was a real watershed for many reasons, not least for what was to happen later that evening. The whole of my family came to visit, and they were all crowding awkwardly into my little room.

Then my brother Darren said to me, 'Is there anything that you fancy, Katrina?'

'What sort of thing?' I asked.

'Anything . . . anything at all.'

I couldn't think of anything I'd want, except the obviously impossible, such as an immediate return to full health. So I simply shook my head sadly.

'There must be something,' Darren said, persisting.

'Such as something to eat?' I said.

'Yeah, or anything else. Can I get you something you'd like to eat?'

'All right,' I said, on the spur of the moment. 'How about some prawn balls?'

'*Prawn balls*?' Mum exclaimed.

'That's what I said. I really, *really* fancy some lovely prawn balls.'

Mum said, 'Katrina, how can you ask for prawn balls? You can't even keep down roast potatoes.'

'But I'd love to have some prawn balls. That's what I fancy, Mum.'

Darren said, 'If you fancy them, we'll go and get them.'

So they went off to see if they could find a Chinese takeaway that was still open. They were gone for ages, and I seriously began to wonder if they'd simply given up and gone home. Then there was a noise in the corridor and Darren and the others charged in, triumphantly holding a little paper carrier bag with the name of a Chinese restaurant printed on the side.

Those prawn balls in sweet and sour sauce were the first food I was able to keep down. It became a running joke between us – whenever they came to visit me they brought me a bag of prawn balls.

Now prawn balls are full of batter and fat. How could they stay down when nothing else would? It doesn't make sense, but for a while that was the only food I could eat.

It was becoming obvious to us all that little Janine was missing her mummy. Mum had been with me at the hospital almost exclusively for three months. She had hardly been home at all, had been away not only from Dad but from her other children too. One day Janine came over to visit me in Oxford and when it was time to leave she didn't want to go. In fact, she made it clear she wanted to stay the night. Well, it's a hospital and not a hotel, and they don't have facilities for guests. Anyway, Janine was then so tiny, unable to fend for herself.

The nurses were very nice to her, and they said Janine could stay for one night only. This was a day when in fact I had been extremely ill, and she had spent much of her time holding sick bowls for me. One of my lines had started bleeding, and Mum had had to rush out to find a nurse to help us. While I was alone with Janine she simply held on to me, keeping the sick bowl under me. I was so wretched.

She said, 'What else do you want, Katrina? Can I get you some water? I'll find you a tissue because you're dripping on your chin.' She was amazing.

But that night, Janine herself started feeling ill. We had already worked out with the hospital that it would be all right for Janine to share Mum's mattress for the night, but as the evening went on she became unwell. The nurses decided that the best thing would be to put her in the room next to mine, which happened to be empty that night, and so they dosed her up with Calpol for her high temperature. She was actually just a short distance away from me. We could see each other through the glass partition separating us. She kept being sick. Poor Mum now had two patients to concern her. She spent most of that long night running between the two rooms.

The main thing I had to put up with in the John Radcliffe was the absence of anyone I could talk to. Yes, it was a lovely hospital and the nurses took a lot of care over everything they did. They treated me like family. They were always going out of their way to help me, would give me almost anything I wanted. If I decided I could eat something they would get someone to go down to the kitchen to make it.

Even so, I was on a children's ward and most of the other patients were babies. There was no one my own age I could talk to. The only person I had was Mum. I'm not criticizing her – I can't, because she gave up her own life for me for all those weeks and months – but we weren't compatible in everything. For instance, she *loves* Cliff Richard! She'd put on her video of Cliff Richard in concert, and I'd think, 'Oh no. Not Cliff again.'

It was a sort of joke between us in the end, but I still had to put up with the video!

She was as trapped in that room as I was, so whenever it was at all possible we tried to get out with the wheelchair for a few minutes. Mum would set up one drip on one side, the second drip on the other, then push me along with her fingers keeping all the lines in place.

One day we were on our way down to the little shop on the main hospital concourse. I was getting addicted to *Take a Break* magazine. I was doing their competitions all the time – I had so much free time on my hands.

We called the lift and Mum wheeled me in. Unfortunately the lift door closed before Mum had got all my drips in with me, and it closed with one of them still outside! So she had no alternative but to block the door with her body, really pushing hard, while she managed to get the drip in with us. It doesn't bear thinking about what might have happened to me if the lift had gone down while I was still attached.

I felt as if I was on the drips the whole time, but there were short periods when they took me off. It was heaven when they did.

Sometimes they would say, 'Katrina, we're going to give you an hour's break.'

I can't tell you how good that felt, not to have the tubes attached! I used to lie down, turning on my side, just for the luxury of being able to do so.

Chapter 9

A few of my friends at school wrote to me while I was in the worst period of the chemotherapy; their messages came to me like signals from an alien world. But they all said they were working hard, studying for their GCSEs.

It made me remember that this was what I would be doing, if I hadn't been taken ill. Only a few weeks before, the prospect of the GCSEs had been looming over me and I too had been studying hard. I'd look at the letters from my friends and think, 'That should be me as well.'

We had obviously informed the school about what was happening to me, but now we told them that I wouldn't be able to attend the exams.

They said, 'Well, all is not lost. You've already done a great deal of course work, and that counts towards the final result. We could submit that on its own.'

I agreed to that. After all, there wasn't much alternative. But I wasn't hopeful about the results and I resigned myself to having to take the exams the next year.

That wasn't what I wanted. I had been hoping to leave school as soon as possible. I'm a materialistic person. I wanted to get away from school, buy my own home, get married. I badly wanted to have a family. I was brought up in a big, busy, happy family, and it was a great environment to be in. I wanted to be like my mum, and if I was going to turn out like her then that was something that would make me happy.

So these occasional letters from my friends had an effect on me. They also reminded me of what I was missing. They would talk about meeting boys, and going to nightclubs. One friend told me at great length about her really nice new boyfriend. I was happy for her but it underlined the fact that I had never had a boyfriend, not in the way she was describing. I couldn't go to nightclubs. I'd spent most of my childhood thinking I was missing out on things – now I knew I was.

I had been in the Radcliffe for more than four months by this time, and had only been home for short periods on about three or four occasions.

Mum said one day, 'I've asked the nurse if you could come home for a few days. You know, another little break.'

The nurses said it was fine by them, but the consultant had his reservations.

'No, I'm sorry, Mrs Leeder. Katrina's not well enough to go home.'

Mum said, 'You know, I really feel it would benefit her to go home for a while. But if you say no, then fair enough, I understand.'

I'd always found this consultant a difficult man, rude even. His medical skills were obviously first-rate, but as far as his tact towards patients went, he had much to learn. He almost never offered praise. He would walk suddenly into my room and say, 'Why are you still in bed?'

On the other hand, if he came in and saw me out of bed, he'd never say, 'Oh, it's good to see you out of bed, Katrina.'

I think he was quite a negative man because he never showed any positiveness towards me. It was always criticism, complaints, warnings. He almost never congratulated me when things went well.

Eventually, I did go home for a few days, and I had a fabulous time. I wanted to go out for a car-ride. It was late in the evening but I was desperate to be driven somewhere – I'd been cooped up in a room for so long. I went out with my brothers Darren and Fenton, and they drove me round the centre of Milton Keynes, just looking at things. We went past a nightclub, with its multi-coloured electric sign, and we drove round the cinema and the shops, seeing the ordinary sights.

We ended up in a little bar in one of the hotels and I met some of my friends there. It was wonderful – I really felt I was somebody again.

Next day, though, it was back to hospital to face the consultant.

The nurse weighed me and found that over the week-end I had lost a tiny amount of weight. It was almost literally nothing – a couple of ounces.

The consultant blew his top. He blamed my mum. He collared her in the corridor outside my room, and tore her off a few strips. He must have known I could hear everything.

His first words were, 'Now, look!' I can't remember the exact words of the rest, but he said something like, 'You've signed Katrina's death warrant now. There's no way that she is going to be well enough to have chemotherapy tomorrow morning. I'm sorry, but you have interfered with our entire plan of treatment.'

All I could think was that my mum didn't deserve a word of it. She had been there with me for four months, helping me; she had never left me there on my own. He had never been there when I wanted to pull my line out, or all the times I wanted to give up, or when I cried, all the times I wanted to go the toilet and couldn't. He was out being a consultant somewhere else, but Mum was there for all of it. Everything she'd done was in my best interests. She knew me; he never did. He had never even bothered to spend a couple of minutes with me trying to get to know me.

So, when I heard him running my mum down I was upset. A few minutes later she came back into my room.

She said to me, 'Come on, Katrina. Out of bed. We're leaving here tonight.'

'What d'you mean we're leaving?' I said.

'He's refusing to give you chemotherapy tomorrow. Well, I'm going to get it. Don't you worry. I'll get you your chemo.'

'Mum, you know no one else can treat me,' I said.

'We're certainly not staying here a moment longer.'

In a little while we'd packed our bags. I couldn't believe it. We phoned a friend of my parents' called Ken, Dad being at work at that time, and Ken came down to Oxford to collect us.

I stayed at home that night. First thing in the morning, we went to Milton Keynes Hospital, and I went to see the consultant there.

After the inevitable blood test he said, 'You're well enough for chemotherapy today. We'll give you what you need.'

They had to obtain the chemo from somewhere else, because the kind I was using was unusual, so I believe the actual course did not start until the day after. From then on I stayed at Milton Keynes Hospital. We found the regime there much more relaxed. They would start me on the chemotherapy, monitor me for a couple of days, then allow me to go home. The only restriction was that I mustn't have contact with anybody. Three weeks later I would return to hospital for the next lot.

It wasn't all plain sailing. The restriction on meeting people was to protect me as far as possible from catching infections. Even so I did go down with illnesses several times. Someone might walk in with a tiny cold sore on their lip or a sniffle in the nose. If that got to me I could easily develop pneumonia.

It's still the same today, but I'm a lot better than I was. I've been told that working at an airport is not exactly the right environment for someone with my health, because of all the germs that go round. I was on the check-in desk recently and a woman passenger came to check in; she was sneezing and spluttering all over the place. I took a tea-break, and let someone else take care of her.

In effect I no longer have a reliable immune system. All I have is the protection afforded by taking penicillin and other antibiotics. I have to be really careful.

After I moved back to Milton Keynes Hospital, life was greatly improved for me. There were still long periods when it was hard to keep my spirits up. Everything seemed to be against me. I cried a lot, but in between those bursts of outwardly visible emotion I just felt endlessly low.

But there continued to be setbacks.

One day I was upstairs in the bathroom and my nose started bleeding. The blood was pouring out everywhere, and I called for Mum. She came running up the stairs and I heard her calling, 'Don't worry darling, you have nosebleeds all the time. You'll be all right.' As she came in through the door she said, 'Oh my God!'

In the few seconds it had taken her to get up the stairs I had spilled blood everywhere. It was all over the tiles, the floor, in the basin and in the bath.

'Why didn't you say it was *serious*?'

'I tried,' I said, indistinctly.

'You're not pinching your nose,' she said, and did it for me.

With that the blood burst out of my mouth.

Dad was at work. Mum ran next door to our neighbour Janet and asked for her help. The next thing I knew, Janet came rushing into the bathroom with a bag of frozen peas.

'These will stop the flow,' she said. 'My David has nosebleeds all the time.' Then she saw the mess. 'Oh my God! What's going on here?'

Mum telephoned the hospital. They said, 'There's no time to order an ambulance. Can you bring her straight down to Casualty by car?'

We already knew that Milton Keynes Hospital didn't have my type of blood in store, but they said they would order some straight away from Oxford, and have it motorbiked over.

This was a period of our lives when my family were living for a short time in Northampton, quite a long drive from Milton Keynes. Because we were expecting to return to Milton Keynes in the near future, and because my medical history was known at the hospital there, that was where I continued to go for all my treatment. We climbed into the back of Janet's Renault 5, with me wrapped in towels and clutching a washing-up bowl. Blood was still pouring out of me, slopping into the bowl.

The hospital had said to my mum that on no account was she to let me fall unconscious, that if I showed any sign of it she was to shake me. So all the way down to Milton Keynes Mum was shaking me and talking to me. I wasn't passing out, but because of all the towels and the blood I could hardly answer.

As we were going down the motorway we heard a hooting sound. There was a car driving abreast of us with four lads inside, and one of them must have spotted the blood. They probably assumed I'd been in a punch-up, and they began waving to us and trying to race our car.

'Oh bloody hell!' Janet said, trying to ignore them.

Fortunately we turned off not much later, and lost the lads. A few minutes later we reached the hospital, and I went into treatment immediately.

Afterwards, the staff said to Mum that if we had been five minutes later I probably wouldn't have made it. I had suffered a major haemorrhage. Fortunately, the blood from Oxford had arrived at the hospital at just about the same time as we did, so they were able to put me straight on to the first of several transfusions.

I don't actually remember too much of what happened that night in hospital, because I drifted in and out of consciousness for hours.

Although I've suffered from nosebleeds most of my life, this one was exceptional. It was caused entirely by the chemotherapy. I had been feeling OK after the most recent dose of chemo, but no matter what else, the treatment knocks your blood count really low, platelets included. Blood is made up of three different kinds of cell: red cells which carry oxygen, white cells which fight infection, and the platelets, which clot your blood. Chemotherapy tends to kill all three kinds.

A few days after my nosebleed I was having one of these low days when I was visited by my brother Darren and his wife Suzanne. I had been told that morning I had lost even more weight, and things weren't looking good.

Darren and Suzanne said they were going to Butlin's for a week.

I said, 'You don't know how much I wish *I* could go to Butlin's!'

'Then why don't you come with us?' Darren said impulsively.

I gestured hopelessly at all my drips and tubes and monitoring equipment.

'I can hardly even go to the toilet on my own,' I said. 'How could I ever get to Butlin's?'

They both looked intently at Mum.

'We could take her!' they said. 'We don't mind. We'd cope somehow. It would give her a break.'

'Well, I don't know,' Mum said. 'I know it would be good for her, but . . .'

'I'm not due to have any more chemo for a while,' I said. 'It's at least another two weeks before it has to start again. The doctor told me yesterday.'

'All right,' Mum said, 'I'll ask the consultant.'

I felt absolutely thrilled by the idea of a week away from hospital, but at the same time I suspected there was no way on earth they'd let me go to Butlin's after what had just happened.

As soon as she could, Mum went and spoke to the consultant about it.

'No, I'm sorry,' he said, 'it's out of the question. Of course she couldn't go to Butlin's. It would be ridiculous.'

Mum said, 'Look, I spend day in and day out with her. I see everything she's going through. You only see her for a few minutes every day. She really feels she's dying and she feels she's stuck in this one place, that there's no end, there's no light at the end of the tunnel. She can't see a future for herself. I believe this would be of great benefit to her to go to Butlin's for five days.'

He wouldn't hear of it, no matter what.

But the nurses were different – they all thought it was a brilliant idea.

It turned out that the consultant's main concern was the Hickman line that went into my chest. This was in place because the large number of injections I was receiving, including the chemotherapy injections, created a danger of my veins collapsing. A lot of the medicines were therefore injected into me through the Hickman line, so it was left in place permanently. Monitoring the line was the most important thing that needed doing, and it had to be done correctly. If anything went wrong with that it could harm me.

They had already trained my mum to flush the line through, which had to be done nearly every day. Mum had to know how to do it in case I was allowed home for a weekend.

One of the nurses said, 'I think it's a great idea. If we could train your brother, or your sister-in-law, to check that line, then I think we can let you go for a week.'

'Really?' I said, hardly believing what she was saying.

'Don't worry, Katrina. We'll talk to the consultant.'

I don't know what they said to him, but the amazing upshot was that he said yes. So the following week I went to Butlin's with Darren and Suzanne. My mum showed Suzanne how to look after the Hickman line. Obviously, I had to be in a wheelchair most of the time, but that was nothing compared with being stuck in a small hospital room for twenty-four hours a day.

Darren folded the wheelchair into the back of his car and we set off for Minehead in Devon. Darren wheeled me around in the wheelchair all week. I went on the Donkey Derby, watched all the swimming and games and dancing, I even started eating. I had some popcorn, I ate a couple of hot dogs.

Part of the reason for this, I think, was that because food wasn't on my mind, it wasn't an issue any more. In hospital, they were always getting at me about food: 'You must eat, you must. Just eat anything.' But now I was on holiday and I wasn't thinking about food like that. I was having as much fun as was possible under the circumstances.

Suzanne was, I think, really nervous of dealing with my line. Who wouldn't be? But that was really the only reminder of my hospital days. Generally, I had a wonderful time. It was one of the first occasions since the beginning of the illness that I actually felt I was a somebody again and not something from outer space.

Even so, a few people did look at me differently. This was the only problem I was aware of while I was at Butlin's. It was the first time I had been out for a long time. I wasn't wearing a wig and of course I was completely bald. Some people cannot help staring. I heard one lot of starers saying, 'Oh, I wonder what's wrong with him?'

They were so insensitive that they could not see past the bald head. I also found that when these people stared at me, or I caught them staring, they wouldn't look away. They kept on staring. Still, I didn't let anything like this spoil the week. But at the end of the week I had to go back to hospital, where they found I'd put on a couple of pounds.

'This is marvellous, Katrina,' they exclaimed. 'Look at you, what have you been eating?'

'Oh, popcorn and hot dogs,' I told them.

Actually, they didn't care what I'd been eating. All that mattered to them was the fact that I'd put on a little bit of weight. What mattered to me was that I came back from the holiday feeling a bit more like a human being again. I was talking and coming out of my shell, emerging from under that black cloud of depression and despair.

But new and different problems always kept on coming at me. I learned I had to be careful about my feet, after what happened when they gave me the chemo.

All through this aftermath of the first big operation, my feet were in a really bad state. The pain and discomfort were continual. Overall, I was getting better, even though it was extremely slowly. Once I started attending Milton Keynes Hospital I was able to walk, talk, write, eat. Normality was inching back towards me. But I could only walk on tiptoes. One day the physiotherapist came in and said, 'Why are you walking like that?'

'Because I had a bad reaction to the chemotherapy.

The only way to keep the pain down is to walk on tiptoes.'

The physio examined my legs closely, pulling and tensing them gently.

'The problem is,' she said eventually. 'Because you've been doing that the tendons in the backs of your legs haven't been stretched. You've been walking like that for five months. The tendons haven't stretched, they've gone and shrunk. If you're ever to walk normally again we're going to have to stretch those tendons.'

She began a course of massage and manipulation, pushing my feet up to try and get them back to a ninety-degree angle to my legs. This went on for ages but, no matter how many times she tried it, as soon as I went to bed, or relaxed in some other way, the feet would flop down.

Whenever I walked it felt most natural, and most comfortable, to lift up on to tiptoes.

One day they took plaster-casts of my legs while two doctors held my feet at the ideal angle, and used them to make some plastic moulds. I was supposed to wear these moulds day and night. The idea was that they would physically hold my feet at the correct angle, causing the tendons to stretch back to normal.

The problem was that the moulds were seriously uncomfortable to wear. They made me sweat because of the plastic pressing against my flesh, and furthermore I couldn't wear them with a skirt. I had to put on trousers all the time. Then I found it was impossible to get my own shoes to fit any more. I was normally a size six, but now I had to get some size eight trainers. I felt I was walking around with my feet inside great boats.

After a while it was clear the moulds weren't working, because my feet were stronger than the mould and no matter how I tied the plastic panels across my feet, still I was trying to walk on tiptoes. My feet kept flicking out of the moulds.

In the end, they decided they would have to put my feet in plaster casts all the time. They used a series of wedges of graduated sizes, which they changed every couple of weeks. Meanwhile, my legs were encased in plaster to keep them rigid. For several weeks I had to go around with these plaster casts on the whole time. They were extremely uncomfortable. Walking was difficult enough, but taking a bath . . .

I wasn't supposed to get the casts wet, so to take a bath I had to use a deckchair while I was in the tub. I would sit in this, with a black plastic sack covering each of the casts. I had to wear a hat on my head so I could tie my little tube up away from the water. Mum would then shower me with the spray, but I wasn't allowed to get my line wet so I had to put a large waterproof patch over that first, tie the tube to my hat, plaster cast on each leg, black sack on each cast. It was horrendous.

In the end, they took the casts off. They simply didn't work. Well, they worked for a while, but my feet kept going slack and I was back on tiptoes again.

'We're going to invest some money in you,' they said

finally. 'There are some orthopaedic boots that we're going to try on you. They cost about £200 a pair. They look like ordinary boots, so you can wear them when you go out.'

From the way they described them I imagined them as slim leather boots, sensually hugging my thighs. When I went to collect them though, my first thought was, 'Oh, you must be having me on.'

They were like moon boots: huge black things with thick straps across them, and they were made with hinges. Whenever I wore them I had to move my ankles in a certain way because of the hinges. Although at first they were indescribably uncomfortable and made me walk as if I really was wading through dust on the moon, in the end they were the answer to the problem. I was soon used to them, and eventually they corrected my feet.

Chapter 10

Bit by bit I was recovering from the physical onslaught of the massive operation and the more insidious poisons of chemotherapy. Bit by bit I was returning to the human race.

There came a point later in 1991 when I wasn't undergoing chemo all the time. There were spaces between, when I was at home, and gradually those spaces were getting longer.

The main cause for concern then was the fact I was not putting weight back on as quickly as they expected. To me there was no mystery: the chemo put me off my food.

The first dose always made me feel sick for the first week, and during the second week I developed painful ulcers in my mouth. The third week was about the only time I had when I felt I could recuperate or get some food down me. In that one week I couldn't put on enough weight to make up for what was going to happen the next time they gave me chemo.

Gradually, though, they extended the periods between doses, and just as gradually my tiny weight began to increase. During those same breaks in the chemo my hair would make a start at growing back. I found this pleasing, because it proved to me that given half a chance it would grow back on its own.

No matter how many times my mum had said in the past, 'It will grow back, Katrina, I promise you,' I had to see it for myself.

The odd thing about this re-growth was that on one occasion the fluff appeared with a reddish tinge; this hair all vanished with the next lot of chemotherapy. The next time it started growing it was jet black. That too quickly fell out, and the next time it was fair.

Clearly it was more than my immune system that was going into a state of nervous collapse from all the chemo I was being given. My hair did grow back blonde in the end, but that was many months ahead.

Before that, in August 1991, my sister Vanessa got married. She wanted me to be a bridesmaid and I wasn't going to let anything stop me. There was only one problem, something I felt very strongly about. It was Vanessa's big day and there was no way I was going to take any of the attention away from her by appearing in a wheelchair with my bald head. I was determined to find the strength to walk, and I did, though I was a bit wobbly on my feet. And my head was covered with a wig made from my own hair. For a day I felt normal again.

I'll never forget my last day of chemotherapy. It was

at the beginning of December 1991, exactly a year since I had first been diagnosed with cancer.

I remember walking into hospital and I could smell that awful, familiar hospital smell. I've always loathed that smell. But this time it barely mattered. I walked in with two friends called Karen and Marie, my mum and my little sister Janine, and I knew that the long and terrible process was coming to an end.

It's difficult to put it into words, but at the heart of it was the knowledge that when I walked out I would be a free woman again, able to get on with being a human once more. I didn't care that I was going to be throwing up for a few days, that for a few more days after that I'd have a painful tongue and gums. This was my last lot!

Everything was healing nicely, the staff had told me. All the scans and X-rays showed a complete remission. No trace remained of the cancer.

It was difficult, looking back, to realize that a whole year had gone by. While I was going through the ordeal it had felt as if it would never finish, that I was in a tunnel where no light showed anywhere, least of all at the end. I had often believed there was no hope, no point of going on. But when I looked back it felt like a year that had sped by.

Oddly, I felt rather isolated by this. I wanted to say to everyone, 'Look at me, I've had cancer. Look at me now, though, I'm fine!'

In the hospitals I had always been surrounded by other sick children, and as far as I could see many of them were very ill indeed. I didn't know anybody who had got better from the illness I'd had. A full recovery was exceptional, but all it did was restore me to the world. It didn't add any special quality to me.

So what was next?

This picture was taken in November 1990. I was sixteen and I had cancer but didn't know it. *(Above)*

I was allowed out of hospital for Christmas. As always, Dad dressed up as Santa. *(Above right)*

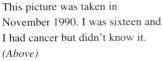

Sunday, 20 January 1991. The night before my operation, Janine kissed me goodbye. *(Above)*

February 1991. Mum insisted on taking this picture, even though I hated the way I looked, telling me one day I'd be glad she did. I didn't feel like smiling but I managed. *(Left)*

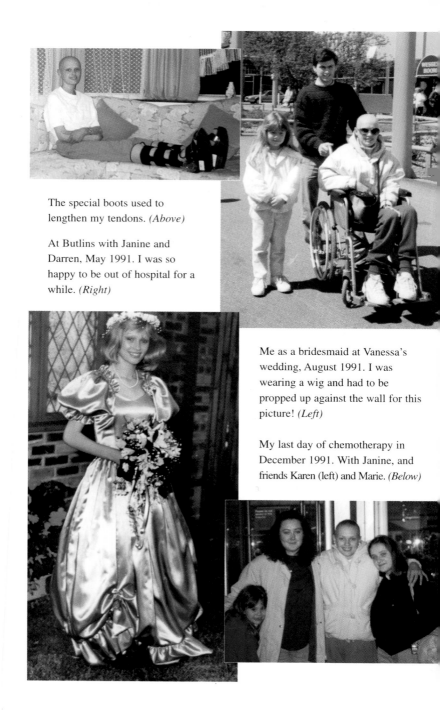

The special boots used to lengthen my tendons. *(Above)*

At Butlins with Janine and Darren, May 1991. I was so happy to be out of hospital for a while. *(Right)*

Me as a bridesmaid at Vanessa's wedding, August 1991. I was wearing a wig and had to be propped up against the wall for this picture! *(Left)*

My last day of chemotherapy in December 1991. With Janine, and friends Karen (left) and Marie. *(Below)*

Julian and I got engaged on New Year's Eve, 1997. When we got home we took this photograph. (*Left*)

On holiday in Tunisia with Julian in May 1998. I must have had cancer but didn't know it. (*Below Left*)

Working at the check-in desk for Reed Aviation, June 1998. (*Below*)

With my mum at my hen night, two days before my chemotherapy.

My first day of chemotherapy, second time around, 10 August 1998.

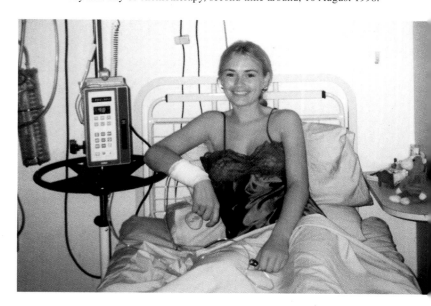

Walking down the aisle, a married woman, with Julian looking proud at my side.

The whole family, from left to right: Janine, Fenton, Mum, Julian, me, Dad, Vanessa, Darren and Tanya.

Mr and
Mrs Batham.
(Opposite page)

Julian and me
cutting the cake
at the reception.
(Above)

In the car on the
way back to
hospital. No one
could have
guessed how ill
I was. *(Left)*

With my surgeon, David Cranston, at the Churchill hospital in October 1998. *(Above)*

Leaving Blenheim ward on 23 September 1998, with my nurse Peter. *(Right)*

With Ross Kemp in February 1999. I sent him this picture when he was in hospital with malaria. *(Below)*

Back at work for Reed Aviation in August 1999. (© London Weekend Television). *(Below right)*

Chapter 11

Pressing in on me was the realization that I had missed a whole year of school. I didn't much relish the thought of returning to school – it felt like a backward step, and after being immobilized by illness for so long I wanted to move *on*.

By this time the results of my GCSEs had come through. I hadn't done too badly, bearing in mind I hadn't sat a single examination, but my course work had always been good and this earned me passes in most of my subjects so all things considered I'd done pretty well.

By February 1992 I was ready to return to school. I still wasn't very secure on my legs, so sometimes I went in my wheelchair. That alone made me feel different from everybody else. I still looked strange too: very thin, pale and frail-looking, with an angular face and bony limbs. Then there was the fact that at least half my friends had moved on. Most of the people I was in school with now didn't know what I'd gone through, or why; many of them didn't even remember me from the old days, when I'd been fit, rounded and blessed with long blonde hair. So I didn't stay long at school, just four months or so, seeing out the school year. My heart was no longer in it.

In the April of that year there had been a welcome interruption. During my chemo year, when I'd been at my worst, I had been approached in hospital by a group called the Make a Wish Foundation. They specialize in the most seriously ill, or terminally ill, children and they come round to you and they offer to grant you a wish. It's called 'Give Kids The World'.

They said to me, 'We grant you three wishes. You pick your first wish. If we can't grant that, we'll do your second or the third. Anything you wish for. And whatever you wish for, you just name it and we'll have it. We'll try our best.'

The idea of the Make a Wish Foundation is to enable sick children either to look forward with hope to something, helping them to get through the illness, or, in the cases where the illness is terminal, to provide an experience that is something they've always wished for.

So I said straight away that I would like to go on a foreign holiday. I'd only ever been to Pontin's or Butlin's, never abroad.

They said, 'Where exactly would you like to go? Disney World?'

'Disney World!' I said. 'Oh, I'd love that!'

It became clear that they thought I should take the trip in the next few weeks. I didn't realize it straight away, but I soon worked out that what they had at the back of their minds was the belief my illness was termi-nal. They were expecting me to die and wanted to give me a brief experience to look back on in my dying days.

They didn't know me. I wanted something to look forward to. So I said, 'No, I'd prefer to go when I'm better.'

It obviously wasn't what they'd had in mind, but after all it was *my* wish they were granting, and that is what I wanted.

By April 1992 I was feeling a whole lot better and the trip to Disney World came round. I went with my mum and dad, my little sister, and my brother Fenton. Fenton came along because as a result of my illness he had become severely depressed. We were all worried about him, and we saw the trip to Florida as a tonic for him as much as for anyone.

Well, we went to Florida and we had a fabulous time. The only problem was that I was still in my wheelchair, but the Disney organization is extremely well prepared for that sort of thing – and anyway, being in the chair always ensured that I went to the front of the queue!

PART TWO
1992–98

Chapter 12

Most of my family have worked for the John Lewis Partnership at some time or another, so when I left school it was for me a natural place to begin my search for a job. There was an added incentive: they had their own drama society.

I have always wanted to be an actress, and in fact before applying to John Lewis I had tried to get into a course at drama school. I can't imagine how I must have seemed to them: when I went in for my audition I could barely walk and was holding on to my tutor's arm for support, I didn't have a hair on my head and I was still as thin as a stick. For the audition I had to read a part from a play, sharing lines with one of the women selectors.

I must have done better than I thought, because somewhat to my amazement I was accepted for the course. Something like two hundred people had applied at the same time as me. I was one of only twenty to be selected. There were snags, though.

Principal among them was the fact that it was a three-year course, and as soon as I was faced with the reality of that I realized it was no longer exactly what I wanted. After my long illness I was desperate to start what I thought of as a normal life.

As I have already said, I'm a materialistic person, and have always wanted a good job, a nice home, as much money as I need. Suddenly the thought of spending another three years, scrimping and saving, getting ready to start a job rather than actually doing one, was too much. Instead, I went for the job at John Lewis, and after the usual panels and interviews, three in all, I was accepted.

I was to spend the next five years working at the John Lewis department store in Milton Keynes. It was a good job, one I thoroughly enjoyed. They put me on a retail training scheme, trying me out in various departments so that they and I could find out what I was likely to be best at. Behind it was a course for an NVQ in Retailing.

I trained first to be a bra fitter, then I moved on to train as a shoe fitter. I had no objections to either of these, but they didn't exactly light up the sky for me. Then they moved me to the unlikely position of selling lawnmowers, and to everyone's surprise, not least my own, I found myself enjoying it.

After I had been away on a retail training course for the products, I worked full-time in the garden machinery department. I loved working there. I can't really say why, except that of all the things in the world lawnmowers were probably furthest from my own interests.

I have never been interested in any kind of gardening, for instance, and I've never been particularly mechanically minded.

What the job really meant, I think, was that when I left it at the end of a day's work I could leave it behind me. I could switch right off. It was also a challenge to me.

It often happened that the customers were men. Most of them took my presence for granted, but a few of them were obviously uneasy by being confronted with a seventeen-year-old girl. Sometimes they would ask, 'Is there a man who can serve me?'

'I'm fully trained to deal with all your enquiries,' I would say. 'May I help you?'

I had to earn their confidence, and that was always a buzz. I knew what I could do, and with a little practice I discovered how to communicate to the customers that I knew my merchandise.

One day I sold the dearest lawnmower in the department. It was the first of its type anyone in John Lewis had ever sold, and it caused such a stir that they featured me in the house magazine. It gave me a real sense of achievement to realize I had done that, I had done it on my own, and I was still only seventeen. When I thought of what I had gone through in the recent past, it was small successes like this that made me feel I was truly recovering.

By this time I had a regular boyfriend who also worked for John Lewis, so for a long time my private and business life very much revolved around the store.

I loved normal life. Even my hair was starting to grow back: it was dark coloured, a long way from my blonde locks of the old days, but I had learnt to count my blessings.

One day my boyfriend and I visited a fairground. After having a few goes on other rides I went on one called *Skid*. As I began to get off the ride they started it up again before I was completely away from it. To my horror my foot was trapped underneath the carriage and I was dragged along for several feet. I was screaming of course, and the man operating the machine quickly put on the brake. By the time I had been pulled clear of the mechanism my foot was hanging limply and I was in terrible pain.

I was rushed to hospital. There they gave me the news that I had broken my ankle. As they put my foot in a cast they advised me to take time off work: at least five and as many as eight weeks would be needed for the fracture to heal properly. It felt to me like another last straw, after all I had been through, to break one of my ankles.

By the time the next morning dawned, I had steeled myself to a new resolve. I wasn't going to allow a small thing like a broken ankle to ruin my life. I still had some crutches, so I went into work that morning on them. I told my department manager what had happened, and pleaded to be allowed to go on working. I told them I would like to work in the office. After a few doubtful glances they managed to arrange this for me. I did my best, but I was never really cut out for clerical work.

After a few days the department manager said to me, 'Katrina, you really shouldn't be working here with your cast on.'

'I can function perfectly well,' I protested.

'Yes, and we aren't criticizing your actual work. But we believe you should be at home resting your foot. As your employers we have your long-term interests at heart. Come back to work when the cast has been taken off.'

We discussed it for a while, but it was clear that this time I wasn't going to have my own way. I'd never had time off work. As I have said, I don't like it, and it's not in my nature. But for all that I finally went home, and spent time uselessly waiting for something to happen. After a couple of weeks I went back to hospital and somehow managed to persuade them that the cast should come off. It was a good few weeks before I was supposed to be free of it. I limped home, and returned to work the next day. Within a couple of weeks my ankle was back to normal.

During my time at John Lewis I was probably a normal member of the staff, despite occasionally surprising everyone with my lawnmower-selling successes. Much of my interest during this period was bound up with the drama society, which I had joined soon after I started the job.

I was involved in several of their performances, and acted in a couple of productions. In one of them I played a drunken nymphomaniac, which I greatly enjoyed doing. There's nothing like acting out of character.

The people in the society were always winding each other up. During the nymphomaniac part I had to take several swigs from a bottle supposedly containing gin. Usually they put water in the bottle, but on the evening of the last performance someone got at the bottle and spiked it. Without telling me they filled it with real gin.

During the play I moved downstage until I was close to the front. As I said my lines I was brandishing the bottle, then finally raised it to my lips and took a swig of it. I gulped a large mouthful of the liquid, realizing too late what it was.

My reaction was unplanned and instant: I spat it out. It sprayed out of my lips and went all over the people in the first two rows of the theatre. As soon as they saw this, everyone at the back of the hall started laughing.

I thought, 'Hello, they like this,' so I did it again. The poor people in the front rows were soaked a second time.

Of course, some of the gin went down, and with no real resistance against neat alcohol I was getting drunk really quickly. I was soon rolling around, giving the performance of my life. My family were there that night, and it's all down on videotape.

Five years soon slipped by. I became an adult, I did well in my job, and I began the long and expensive process of buying a house. It was just a small place, but it was in a quiet backstreet in one of the most pleasant of Milton Keynes's suburbs. My traumatic, illness-shrouded adolescence became increasingly remote from me. Eventually even my hair grew back to its former length, and with that it reverted at last to its natural blonde colour.

Then I met Julian.

I had been with another boyfriend more or less from the time I started work at John Lewis. This first young man was hugely important to me at the time, mainly because out of all the people I met in those post-cancer days he was the first one who accepted me for what I was. I must have been a strange sight when he first met me, as I was just getting over cancer and I hardly had any hair. I knew that wouldn't be for ever, but I was the only one who did. He obviously saw past this, and was prepared to take me as he found me.

By the time I met Julian I had spent four years with my first boyfriend. We had grown steadily together, as I readjusted to the world. I could possibly have done it all without him, I think, but it wouldn't have been so happy, so free of anguish.

We loved each other very much, but I believe he wasn't ready to settle down. I was different: I wanted to build a nest. I felt he was going along with it because he was loyal to me, not because he had the same needs as me. Eventually it was clear to us both that it was not going to work any more, and after much soul-searching, and not a little unhappiness, we decided reluctantly to call it a day.

The same night I popped round to my brother Darren's house. I was obviously upset because of what had just happened, so I wasn't really ready for a change. That's when Julian turned up.

He was a friend of Darren's and he simply turned up at the house while I was there. He had just bought a new car and wanted to show it off to my brother. Darren introduced me to Julian. I think I'd heard of him or about him in the past, from Darren, but I hadn't paid much attention and we had certainly never met in person.

When I met my first boyfriend it was love at first sight, but things were different when I met Julian.

My first impression was favourable, though. I remember thinking, 'Oh, I like him. He smells nice and he looks nice.'

Julian was crisp. That's a word that really describes him: he was crisp. His clothes were neatly ironed, his shoes were polished and his hair was in place. He smelled subtly of aftershave.

As for me, I was feeling far from crisp. In fact, I was in a real state that night. I had been crying and knew that it showed. I was wearing an old brown dress and a pair of elderly socks that were full of holes.

Since I wasn't expecting to get interested in anyone just then I didn't feel too bad about it, but I must say that afterwards I did wonder what sort of impression I had made.

However, that night Julian said to me, 'I hear you're moving house. You're buying somewhere, aren't you?'

I said I was.

'OK,' he replied. 'I'll sort some bits out for you.'

I didn't think too much about this vague offer, but the next day Darren phoned me up.

'Julian's left some things round here for you,' he said. 'You've got an iron and some mugs and lots of other stuff.'

That evening I went round to pick them up. Darren was teasing me a little, saying I ought to give Julian a ring to say thanks.

Without thinking very far beyond that, I phoned Julian the next day. To my amazement he said, 'How about me taking you out for a drink, then?'

I was pleased, but immediately on the defensive.

'To be honest,' I said, 'I've only just come out of a long relationship.'

'Yes, I'd heard.'

Julian told me he'd often seen me around John Lewis with my previous boyfriend.

'I need some time to readjust,' I said. 'I'm not ready for . . .'

'It would be only as friends,' Julian said. 'I understand how you might feel.'

'Well, I don't know . . .'

He was persuasive, though, without building it up too much. Finally I said, 'Oh, all right, then.'

Julian picked me up that evening and the first thing I realized was that of course he could drive and had his own car. This was the first big change; with my previous boyfriend it was me who did all the driving. Being with Julian really felt like being taken out by a man.

We drove over to Northampton, to one of the big pubs there. I was beginning to think how much I liked him, how romantic he was, when he broke the spell.

'You're going to have to buy this round,' he said. 'I

was so worried about being late that I forgot to draw any money out.'

This made me think he wasn't all that serious. He took me home at the end of the evening, though, and asked me out again. I said yes, feeling pretty casual about the whole thing. The habit stuck quickly, nevertheless, and we started seeing each other almost every night. Soon it was more than regular dating.

There came the time when I felt I should tell him about my illness. Not because I wanted to dwell on what had happened, but because there was always that terrifying prospect of the cancer returning one day.

Fortunately, Julian already knew something about my background; Darren must have talked about it. Also, I had sometimes gone to see my brother in Waitrose – where Julian worked with Darren – and Julian had spotted me a couple of times with my hair starting to grow back.

One day I told him everything, but I don't think it sank in. He seemed inclined to treat it as something in my past, and to be honest I preferred him thinking about it that way. That's where the cancer was safest: behind me.

Julian and I brought out the romantic in each other right from the start. We are always doing little things to surprise each other. For example, one day I opened my lunch sandwiches at work and I found that Julian had left a little silk rose in with them.

Perhaps our most romantic moment was when we got engaged.

We had gone down to London to see in the New Year; we wanted to be in Trafalgar Square when Big Ben struck midnight, to be at the heart of it all. From little things that had happened over the previous few weeks and days, I had been hoping that we might get engaged soon, but Julian likes to keep things secret, and I didn't want to spoil things by dropping hints.

We found our way to Trafalgar Square and were standing in the immense crowd.

'Where's Big Ben?' Julian suddenly said.

'It's down there,' I said, pointing along Whitehall.

'Would you prefer to go down there and be near it?'

'Yes.'

So we pushed our way out of Trafalgar Square and walked on down towards the river. We were laughing and joking and at one point I happened to slap against his pocket. I felt something hard there, and immediately I thought, 'That feels like a ring to me.'

I couldn't get it out of my mind. We walked across Parliament Square until we were as close as possible to Big Ben, and I kept thinking about the ring I was certain he had in his pocket. It was nearly midnight, and I knew that if he was going to propose to me he would do it when the clock struck. I kept glancing up at the time. Suddenly, Big Ben started striking and I looked round straight at Julian. He was still standing up! I realized he wasn't going to propose to me after all.

But then he said, 'Is that Big Ben striking?'

'Yeah,' I said.

'It's definitely Big Ben?'

'Yes, Julian,' I told him. 'We're right underneath it.'

How could he not hear it? It was donging really loudly.

'Ah well, I'd better get on with it then,' he said.

He went down on one knee – straight into a puddle – and he proposed to me there and then. Everyone around us was cheering. Julian pulled the ring from his pocket and slipped it on to my finger. I held it up for everyone to see.

'I've just got engaged!' I said in excitement.

All the people clustered around us, slapping us on the back and congratulating us. Someone had a bottle of champagne and they shared it with us, and all I could think about was how wonderful it was to be engaged to this fabulous man, and how perfect it was all going to be.

Chapter 13

After five years at John Lewis I came to the conclusion I needed a change in life. This restlessness might have been cured by simply changing to another department within the store, but at the time I was looking around no vacancies were available.

What I really wanted was to try something new.

About three years earlier a girl I knew at John Lewis had moved to a job at Luton Airport, and when I remembered that and thought about the possibilities, I decided I would try the same. The main appeal of it was that I knew nothing at all about the work, and it would therefore present me with a real challenge.

I telephoned a firm called Reed Aviation. When I'd flown from Luton Airport once before they had checked me in. I had liked the way they handled people and the problems that arose. They seemed extremely professional.

The woman I spoke to at Reed Aviation told me there weren't any vacancies at the time, but said they would keep my application on file. They needed a CV and a recent photograph with the application form, but they were both easy for me to arrange. The application form arrived the next morning and I sent everything back at once. I assumed that would be the last I would hear from them.

To my surprise they called back two days later, asking me to attend an interview. On the appointed day I drove down to the airport, and as soon as I got going I was struck by the commuting distance that was involved. Obviously I had been that way many times in the past, but suddenly I saw that it was going to be twenty-eight miles in each direction, every working day, most of it along the busiest motorway in Britain.

The traffic that particular day was heavy, so I felt I was getting a realistic idea of how difficult the journey was going to be. (In fact, I've since discovered it can be a lot worse.)

Even so, I was early for the appointment. It was inevitable, really – I'm never late. For half an hour I sat in my car reading a magazine. When I left the car and went into the building, I discovered my stomach was tense with butterflies.

The interview was a one-on-one: an extremely pleasant woman made me feel comfortable, encouraging me to be relaxed and normal. The result was that I handled all her questions with great confidence, feeling that everything was going well.

The point of the interview was a general one: it was a chance for us to get to know one another. We talked about what work experience I had had so far, what sort of expectations I had about the job at Reed Aviation, and perhaps while talking she had a chance to assess how much self-confidence I had and how well I might be able to deal with any tricky situations that might arise.

The interviewer made no bones about the fact that it could sometimes be a hard job, not at all suitable for everyone, and that it took special skills to be able to do it successfully.

She told me that it would be six months before I would be entitled to take a holiday, then went into some detail about the shift patterns, making clear what they would be and how they were likely to affect my private life.

Privately, I was thinking to myself how tiring the shifts sounded, but I continued to radiate confidence while the interview continued. By this time I had decided I really did want the job, and that I was willing to give the shifts a try.

I've never been the kind of person who wanted to flit from job to job. I take decisions like that carefully. The woman couldn't have known it but I was capable of making a steady decision.

The whole way through the interview I felt confident, to the extent that afterwards, driving home, I wondered if I might have seemed too confident. That sort of thing doesn't always go down too well.

Three days later the phone went and someone from Reed Aviation told me that I had the job.

At first I couldn't believe it. I had wanted it and I had set out to achieve it, but it was highly satisfactory to be told I'd made it. The only cloud on the horizon was the fact that I had to hand in my notice at John Lewis.

I was sad to do this. The firm encourages the idea of a sense of family amongst its employees, and in my case it was also literally true. Also, five important years of my life had been spent there, those years when I had developed away from my illness-ridden teen years, had met and fallen in love with Julian, bought my first house, and everything else. Leaving John Lewis was *not* easy.

I was crying on my last day there, saying goodbye to everyone, and it was all a huge wrench overshadowed by a sense of the unknown. On the way home, driving a friend back, I asked her, 'Do you think I have done the right thing?'

'Of course!'

'I feel I should go back there and ask them if I can have my job back.'

'Katrina, you've got a new career path opening up,' the friend said, 'All you have to do is follow it.'

'Yes, but . . .'

'Give it a try. If it doesn't work out I know they'll have you back.'

Afterwards, alone, I thought less emotionally about my decision. I decided I was going to make the best of it, was going to like it. I've always been one to make the best of a situation, even when I don't like it.

A couple of days later Julian and I flew off to Turkey for a two-week late holiday. The idea was the same as for many holidays: to have a rest, find a break between two hectic parts of your life. In this sense the first week in Turkey was fine but as soon as the second week was under way I realized I was counting down until the following week. I kept saying to Julian, 'Oh no, there are only eight more days before I start my new job.' Then it was seven days . . . I didn't really enjoy that second week.

As soon as we were back at home I had to start preparing. I was going on a two-week training course, and already I was coming up against a number of rules.

The company put limits on what you could and couldn't wear during the training. For instance, it said that girls had to wear skirts, they had to wear shoes with heels, our hair had to be tied back, we had to wear a certain amount of make-up, we had to wear ear studs and not dangly earrings, only one dress ring and engagement ring or wedding ring was allowed, a watch but no bracelet.

The list was so long that I was worried I was going to wear something that they'd pick me up on and fail me for.

In the morning I left home about two hours too early, to be absolutely sure I was there in time. Inevitably, yet again, I ended up sitting in the car park with about an hour to spare. I read a magazine until the time came, then went across to the building where I had been directed.

I discovered there were other people who would be taking the training with me. I could see straight away they were all as nervous as I was. There was one particular girl who seemed confident, which reminded me of how confident I had been during the interview. Here it was different, though: I was rather lost and didn't know what to do.

I'm very much the kind of person who learns something best by actually doing it. I find it difficult to learn from a book. This was a constant worry for me throughout the training course: they would tell us what we had to know, and hand out information sheets, and I would find it hard to take in. All this changed, though, the moment we were able to put the training into practice after the course itself had finished.

But it was a problem for me during much of the course. For instance, we would learn about everything we had to do when checking in a flight: what differences there were depending on the destination, the nationality of the passengers, and so on. At the end of every day we would go home with a big wad of papers for revision, and the next morning there would be a written test. We had one of these tests every morning for the first week, and I managed to scrape by with results that weren't too bad.

Much of the course, though, was interesting and even pleasant. For instance, there was the day a lady came round to fit us up for our uniforms. When we put them on for the first time we began to feel the part, that we were members of the company staff. We put on our lovely black and red hats, and the skirts and jackets, and by looking the part we began to feel more able to do the job. We even had training in how to put on make-up properly, the sort of thing most young women take for granted that they already understand, but you suddenly realize it is an important part of how the company projects its image to the public.

Some of the training was more technical and practical. One day, for example, they showed us what to look for when someone presents a passport, how to tell a false one from a real one.

At the end of the full course we had to sit one final written test paper. I tried my best but I only just passed.

I spoke to my manager, feeling a bit defensive about the result.

'Look,' I said. 'I know it doesn't seem good, but I know me. Once I put all this into practice, I'll take it in straight away. There'll be no problem. I just need some real experience and it'll be all right.'

Chapter 14

On my first day on duty the supervisor told me to go out and stand behind one of the other girls doing check-in. This particular girl had herself only been working for Reed Aviation for two weeks. There she was, already apparently an expert, and showing me how to check in the passengers for an easyJet flight.

It was such a responsibility but it was also a buzz. The job is an important one, and on the whole the check-in staff have to make serious decisions about letting people on the planes, what they do with their baggage, and so on. And there I was, on my first day, practically doing the job.

Only a few hours later, I really was doing the work on my own. They had no one to open a flight so they asked me to do it. I was painfully aware that I had only been there for one day.

The other girls were supportive. They said, 'Katrina, you have to get used to this. We all get sent out, thrown in the deep end when we least expect it.'

I had thought they were just winding me up, but there it was, really happening. I went out to attend to that flight, thinking hard about what I had to do. I took my notes with me and kept them out of sight under the desk, but as I had known all along, once I was out there really doing the work everything seemed to run all right.

I was obviously slow and super-careful about the work, but I made no mistakes that I was aware of. After a few minutes one of the other check-in girls came over and sat with me.

We were constantly observed while we worked, and the supervisors would pick us up for the tiniest things. All the staff were treated like this, not just me, not just the new girls.

The sort of thing they pointed out would be that we hadn't put enough lipstick on, the message being that we had to go and re-apply it straight away. Another time I was out in the rain pathing the flight; this means having to walk with the passengers out to the aircraft. I was absolutely drenched, so I returned to the terminal with my hat off – it had become soaked while I was outside. I was promptly told to put the hat back on.

The early days passed quickly, and within a week or two I no longer felt so green. All the staff were support-ive, and in spite of what I have been saying about the rules, in practice the management was fair and even-handed. Everything was geared to the smooth handling of the passengers, of projecting a good and professional image.

Working at Luton Airport is in general a great challenge. Every day is different. From one day to the next you never know what kind of passenger you're going to be dealing with, what kind of problem might arise. easyJet caters for both international and domestic flights, and you soon discover that the passengers for the two types of flight are different from each other.

Domestic passengers are usually on business trips. These are the people who are the most likely to give you problems. It's almost always to do with their hand luggage – they frequently try to carry overweight baggage on to the plane because they want to work while the flight is in progress. It's important no one places a single piece of hand luggage weighing more than five kilos into the overhead since if a heavier bag were to fall out it could hurt someone.

I've dealt with quite a few awkward passengers in my time. I must admit that sometimes I get home after keeping my cool all day, and as soon as I'm indoors I find myself starting to cry. It all just wells up. It's almost always because of some passenger giving me trouble over something to do with the ticket, the passport or the baggage.

At the end of my first full week, I told my mum that I wasn't enjoying it as much as I thought I would.

'You'll settle down, Katrina,' she said, calmly.

She was right. After about a month I began to feel happy in the job, and I still do. Two years later I can say honestly that now I really enjoy my job, and can take the rough with the smooth.

Sometimes the rough can be pretty hard to deal with,

though. You hear a lot about air-rage these days, but in my experience ground-rage is just as common and sometimes just as serious. I've had to cope with some really difficult passengers. One woman hit me on the arm, I've been sworn at more times than I can remember, and somebody once spat at me. I've even had bags thrown at me – and that was by a vicar!

Part of the solution to this is being able to spot in advance which of the passengers are going to be trouble. You can't always tell, though. I always remember one man whom I had to charge for excess baggage. He grumbled and complained, but I managed to stay calm and explain to him why the extra charge was being made. He quietened down, I completed checking him in, and he moved away from my desk. I thought that was the end of the matter.

A few minutes later, though, he was back. This time he pushed a large bar of chocolate across the desk towards me.

'That's for you,' he said, a little gruffly.

I started to explain that it wasn't necessary, but he immediately interrupted me.

'I didn't like having to pay extra for my baggage,' he explained. 'But you were so calm and professional that in the end I didn't mind.'

It would therefore be completely wrong to give the impression that all passengers are trouble. The vast majority of people pass painlessly through the process. Of course, it's the troublesome ones you tend to remember most.

My experience with John Lewis has actually been a great help to me, when it comes to handling difficult passengers. A complaining customer there generally has his side taken up by the management.

At an airport the set-up is a little bit different from that in a department store. The emphasis is not on selling, but on safety precautions, security systems, the sheer logistics of moving thousands of different people through a complicated series of procedures to their aircraft. In a shop someone goes in to buy something; at an airport you have passport controls, customs, ticketing, baggage, shops, lost children, drunks, late arrivals, delayed departures, bad weather – any or all of these things. To ensure smooth working there are a huge number of commonsense rules.

If any people try to bend those rules, or want to change things around to their own personal advantage, they're going to need a *very* good reason to do so. Otherwise, the answer is no. So if a passenger gives a checking assistant a hard time the managers will usually stand up for the check-in system, and back their staff.

Sometimes an aggressive passenger won't take no for an answer from a check-in girl, but demands to see a supervisor. This happens frequently in times of stress. More often than not the supervisor will only repeat what I've just said, simply because it is the only thing that can be said, but because it comes from somebody the passenger knows is in a higher position than me it gets taken more seriously.

I must emphasize, though, that these troublesome

passengers are the minority. We do have some lovely passengers. Sometimes when it happens to be quiet and there's not much happening around the desks we get a chance to chat to some of the passengers.

I still receive letters from a lady who is travelling the world. She left Luton Airport two years ago on her way to France. Since then she has travelled to about six more countries, and writes to me from wherever she happens to be. This is all because we had a chance to chat at the check-in desk for about twenty minutes.

I've had passengers come over to see me when they've landed back at Luton, and they want to say hello before they leave the airport, because they got to know me when they were checking in on the outward flight.

I know I am resilient to the harder side of the work, because I feel that over the years I've learnt to be a fighter. I persevere with a problem and I'll take something on. I'll always see something through to the end, I'm not one to give up on anything. And at the same time I'll look for the best in a situation.

Take the problem of the shifts, for example. When I first began working at Reed Aviation the first four or five months were, I must admit, very hard. I worked four days on and two days off. This doesn't sound too bad, until you think of the hours involved.

I started work at the airport at five in the morning. That meant I had to get up at about three o'clock because it takes me an hour to get ready, bathing and dressing. Then I would leave my house at about four o'clock to get into the airport before five. I would finish work at about half-past two or three o'clock. By the time I had driven home it would be gone four o'clock. I'd be worn out, and so I'd doze for a bit then fall fast asleep. The next thing I knew it would be three in the morning again, and another day was beginning.

It was extremely hard to live with. All my sleep patterns were upset, so I'd be really sleepy when I was awake and only able to sleep fitfully when I went to bed. Then there was the problem of Julian coming in from work, finding me wanting to sleep when he was just winding down from his own job. Sometimes we'd have dinner together and then I'd find it hard to sleep on a full stomach. Or else I'd actually be asleep and he would wake me up by having the TV on downstairs.

In fact there were two shift periods: what we called the earlies and lates. In some ways the lates were even harder than going to work in the small hours: they ran from something like half-past two in the afternoon until midnight. I would get home at some unearthly hour of the morning, one o'clock, or some time close to that, tired out but wide awake. Julian would obviously be in bed by then, but I would need to wind down and have a chat, so then I'd wake him up. It wasn't easy for either of us.

So the shift pattern really did take a toll at the beginning.

Like everything else connected with the job, the worst came first. The shift patterns aren't so difficult to live with now that I've been with the firm for more than two years. I currently work three days on, three days off:

twelve hours at a time, but usually during the daylight hours.

It's still a long day – we only get an hour for lunch in the middle of that – but knowing that I have three full and uninterrupted days to come afterwards makes it easier to live with.

So, after two years I found myself one of Reed Aviation's longer-serving employees. Because the job is hard for some people, and the shifts are so tough, most people don't stick at it. And for others there are always the temptations of moving on: for instance, the chance of applying to join cabin crew or taking the even harder route upwards into management. But I was happy with what I was doing and in spite of the problems I had settled down and life was on an even keel.

But things were shortly to change dramatically. In one sense the upheaval began one day when I heard a rumour that a TV company was going to make a documentary at Luton Airport, and that of all the airlines using the airport they had chosen easyJet.

PART THREE
1998

Chapter 15

The news about the TV filming was at first just a rumour, but it was soon confirmed. Stelios Haji-Ioannou, the chief executive of easyJet, had given it his approval. As easyJet is one of the main companies handled by Reed Aviation it meant all the staff were likely to be involved in the programme. When you learn this sort of thing you can't help feeling interested.

One day in the middle of June 1998 I was sitting in the Reed Aviation office and someone came in and mentioned that several members of a camera crew were filming outside. They had arrived without any fuss and were getting down to it straight away. Later, when I went out, I saw that they were filming one of my colleagues, an assistant supervisor called Jane.

I went to work on my check-in desk, and one of the production team wandered over to me and started chatting. It was all extremely informal, and as I saw the film crew going about their job they seemed a friendly bunch. At this stage they weren't filming me, and I saw comparatively little of them.

Two of my days off then came along, and when I

returned to work later in the week one of the managers told me they wanted me to go on a new training course. With Reed Aviation being a handling agent we have to work for many different airlines, and for each airline we have to learn their particular ways of doing things.

The new airline was Jersey European and I jumped at the chance. I always enjoy learning new things, so I said yes straight away. The course was due to begin the following Thursday.

Before then I had three more days off, and on the Monday I was due to go for one of my regular hospital check-ups.

These had been going on ever since the chemotherapy had finished and with time had become routine. Julian had never been with me on one of these visits, and because this time they would be doing an ultrasound scan I had suggested he might come along to see what happened.

When I went to hospital I was feeling no more apprehensive than usual – for who can go for tests at a hospital without even a shadow of worry? But I had no especial fears about what the doctors might discover.

A few months earlier I might not have felt so calm. The previous December I had been feeling very ill indeed. I had suffered symptoms that were alarmingly similar to the ones I'd had when the cancer had first been detected. I couldn't understand why I was being sick and feeling so faint. Also, my stomach was hard and sometimes in the mornings it would feel and look swollen. I was putting on weight.

I had gone to see my doctor and he decided that I had a water infection and gave me a course of antibiotics. I wasn't too happy with that, convinced it was more serious, so I consulted another doctor. This one told me that I was being paranoid; the cancer was definitely not returning. I asked him if he would arrange an ultrasound scan, just to reassure me, but for some reason he would not. I had assumed that my medical history would have assured me of a scan whenever there was the slightest doubt, but apparently not.

In any event it did turn out to be just a scare. Within a few weeks the symptoms had cleared up, and by February of that year I wasn't worried any more. I knew I was due to have a routine scan on 22 June, and that if there were any problems they would be picked up then. So by the time this regular visit came around I felt no more worries than usual about my health.

Julian was in the room with me when the scan began, and because I had known the doctor for several years we were joking with him as he began the test. All of a sudden, though, I saw the expression on his face change. I noticed at once; instantly I felt a tremor of alarm. Because we had so recently been joking around with each other, my next thought was that he was trying to wind me up.

But he said, 'Katrina, I'm so sorry. I don't know how to tell you this . . .'

Before he could say any more I burst into tears.

I could see Julian's face – he obviously hadn't realized why I was crying. The doctor was still speaking – I

141

heard the words 'mass' and 'lump' – but I was hardly listening. Fear and anguish were coursing through me. It was the worst of news, the absolute worst.

Just as once before, in similar circumstances, I had clung to the idea that Mum was joking when she told me, so again I snatched at that as the last, desperate hope.

'You're joking!' I cried. 'Tell me this is a joke!'

'I'm not joking,' the doctor said, not looking me in the eyes. 'I'm sorry. I can only tell you what I've found. I can see a mass near to where your left kidney should be.'

'But I don't have a kidney there. It was taken out.'

The tears were really flooding out of me by this time. The doctor only shook his head, not able to give me any reassurance. He simply put his hand lightly on my leg and looked at Julian.

He said again, 'I'm so sorry.'

That's when I finally realized he wasn't joking.

As calmly as possible I said to him, 'What do you think it could be?'

'I can't tell you without giving you a CT scan. But it does look as if your tumour might have come back.'

I couldn't understand, I couldn't take it all in.

I left the hospital room in a daze, holding on to Julian.

Julian said, 'At least he hasn't said definitely it has come back. He only said it might have. It's just a small mass he's seen.'

That was Julian all over, but I'd been in the same situation seven years earlier, and I had a feeling of certainty and familiarity about what was happening to me.

I remembered what had happened to me the previous December, the doubts I had had then. No news the doctors could give me would be good news: there was no such thing as a little cancer, a mild form of tumour.

Doctors are like everyone else, in that they find it difficult to say the harshest words. I knew with every bone in my body what those words ought to be, that my cancer was back. It was back, and this time it was going to be worse.

The doctor had advised me to take a couple of weeks off work, time to get used to the idea, time to clear your mind, he said.

He didn't know me very well. Time off work was the last thing I wanted then.

I went straight round with Julian to see Mum.

Julian was still trying to put the news in what he saw as proportion.

'Pauline,' he said to Mum. 'All the doctor has found is a mass. It's not definite yet.'

Mum and I looked at each other, a terrible familiarity lay between us, forged in those long months of my earlier illness.

'It's cancer again,' I said. 'I know it is, Mum.'

'Look, Katrina, until it's completely definite, we mustn't decide anything.'

'You didn't see the doctor's face!' I said. 'I know what this is, I know what it is!'

'I wish I knew what to say,' she said, and we held each other closely. I was crying again.

The hospital phoned up and said they'd fixed an

appointment for me to have a computed tomography scan, a CT scan, on the Wednesday. That alone told me it was serious: there was usually a long waiting list for those.

Julian wasn't working in the morning that day, so he and Mum came in with me while I had the scan.

I always hate these scans. You have to lie on a long table, which propels you into a device which looks rather like the front of a washing machine. They use a computerized voice, sounding like a woman, that tells you to breathe in or out at certain times. I've had so many of these scans that I know the routine well.

That morning I was crying as I was drawn slowly along. I was thinking to myself about all the frightening possibilities of what lay ahead.

I knew the doctors were out on the other side, in their little room, reading off the results of the scan as they came through, seeing what was inside me and knowing about it before I did. All I could seem to do was cry and cry, trapped on that long hard bench as it took me through the machine, while I wondered what was going on, what they were seeing, what they were thinking and deciding.

At the end, when I came out, I looked at Mum. After the first illness, when we went through so much together, I knew Mum would never lie to me about my illness, would never try to soften the truth. So I didn't look at the doctors, but turned to my mum.

I wanted the truth, no matter what it was.

'Have I got a tumour?' I said. 'Is it cancer?'

'Yes, darling,' Mum said, 'I'm afraid it is.'

Before any of the doctors could say anything to me I walked straight out and I ran down the hospital corridor. I was crying and crying. I came to a wall and I was about to smack my head hard on it when Julian and Mum caught up with me. Why was it happening again? *Why me*?

We all cried together.

I said, finally, 'Mum, what's going to happen? I can't understand this.'

Eventually I had calmed down enough to let them lead me back to the waiting room. The doctor was there, and speaking quietly and calmly he told me what the scan had revealed. He understood it was another Wilms Tumour, but without a biopsy they couldn't tell for sure. He said they wanted to admit me to hospital for the biopsy.

I couldn't go home. I didn't know what I wanted to do. I walked out of hospital and all I could think was that that word had come back into my head. Death. Cancer meant death. The future had been taken away from me again. I was back in that long dark tunnel without a glimpse of light.

Julian kept saying, 'It's going to be all right, Katrina. It'll be all right.'

He was trying to soothe me, but it was hurtful because I felt he was being too casual about it. I knew, really, he wasn't being casual at all. He hadn't been through it before, didn't know what was involved, what was going to *happen*. He had no way of knowing how to deal with the situation. Also, he must have been as scared as me, and not known how to show it, or even whether he should show it at all. It wasn't his fault.

Julian phoned his work and told his manager what we had just been told and that he wouldn't be coming in for the rest of the day. When he came off the phone, it was obvious he had been crying.

Mum lent me the keys to her caravan down in Cosgrove, so Julian and I went there to spend the afternoon together. It was a quiet time together, but at one point, when Julian left briefly to go to the toilet, I was alone. The caravan is by a lake. I stared out over the placid water and I thought to myself, 'When I wake up in the morning I'm not going to be here.'

I was convinced I was going to die that night. It felt as if we had been given one more evening together, then that would be it.

As we drove home I said to Julian, 'I'm going to get my uniform ready for tomorrow.'

'You can't be serious. You're not going to go back to work after this!'

'I have to, Julian.'

'The doctor said you should take a couple of weeks off.'

'To do what? Sit around thinking about it?'

I knew that the best way to deal with the news was to keep my mind off it. I wanted to cling to normality as long as I could. And not only that – I don't like letting people down. I'd already agreed to start the new training with Jersey European; I knew they needed me. As

146

far as I can I never let other people down. Mum always taught me to treat people the way I would like to be treated myself.

So although Julian was in one important sense right – that I should make myself my first priority – the concerns of the job were not something I could ignore. I had to report to Jersey European the next day.

We discussed it, and I know Julian had a point, but in the end he saw what I wanted. The next day the training began.

One or two of the people commented on the way I looked: my eyes were bloodshot, and I must have had a distracted manner that they noticed. I shrugged it off, saying I hadn't slept well the night before.

There were two other girls on the course with me, and we were crammed together into a tiny office with the training officer. There was the usual amount of hard information to take in, and I dutifully wrote it all down in my notes, but in truth little of it was sinking in.

With only three of us there was nowhere to make myself inconspicuous, so like the other girls I was asked a number of questions by the training officer, and I wasn't able to handle them well. At one point I was asked if I had been listening properly.

I was thinking, 'Please, don't you know I've just been told I have cancer?'

Of course the poor woman couldn't know that. And equally, though for less obvious reasons, I didn't want to tell her or anybody else about it. The truth was that at this stage I felt embarrassed and I didn't want *anyone* to know. I wanted to try and hide the news for as long as possible. I wasn't sure why I felt like that but that's the long and short of it.

Part of it was that I felt as if I had let myself down, but it wasn't only that. When I was on the Jersey European training course, in that tiny room with the others, I had to concentrate on what I was seeing on the computer monitor. It's complicated trying to learn all the ins and outs of one particular company's checking-in procedure. Whenever I looked at that monitor, I found it almost impossible to focus on any of it. I was staring away into nothing.

I knew I wasn't responding as well as I should to the training, so when I got a chance I had a word with my manager. I wanted to tell her what was going on. Word would inevitably filter back to her about the difficulty, and I wanted her at least to know that there was a reason for it.

When it came to the point, though, I found it almost impossible to say the dreaded word. It was like a superstitious naming of names, as if by saying the word 'cancer' it would make my predicament worse.

There was something else too: I felt degraded by having developed the illness again, that the very name of it was embarrassing and dirty to speak. The word exists with so many associations and connotations: everyone has bad thoughts about cancer. I tried to hint to the manager what was going on, hoping she would realize what I was saying, perhaps even utter the word for me, but in the end I had to come out and say it.

Her immediate response was to suggest I should go home, but I said no.

'I have to stay here,' I said. 'I don't want to go home and think about this.'

I went back to training for Jersey European. Emboldened a little by having talked to the manager, I took the training officer aside.

I said, 'Look, I'm not feeling my best today.'

'I realized something was wrong.'

'Please bear with me. I'm awfully sorry.'

'I understand,' she said, although because I hadn't told her everything she couldn't really have done so. 'No problem, Katrina.'

I got through the day.

When I reached home in the evening my mum phoned to say that the hospital had been in touch with her. They wanted me to go in for the biopsy the following week. The appointment happened to fall on one of my work days, which would mean taking the day off. That was the first day I'd had off since I started working for Reed Aviation.

Chapter 16

I returned to work the following week knowing I was going to have to tell everyone that I had cancer. This was one of the hardest things. No one at work knew my medical history – why should they? Now I knew in addition that the illness I had suffered as a child would also undoubtedly come out, as well as this new problem. I felt everyone would look at me differently, see me as somehow dirty.

I kept using that word to describe how I felt. Julian, for instance, couldn't understand why I kept saying I felt dirty. But I was diseased, something big was wrong with me, and it set me apart.

I've experienced the attitude held by many people, in all walks of life, about terminal or incurable diseases. It's something they cannot confront in their own lives. They're scared of the thought. They back away mentally, and it becomes a habit. Then one day they're confronted by someone they actually know and they find out that that person has the very disease of which they are so scared. And they can only deal with it by backing off, trying to make a sick joke of it, gossiping about it.

Someone with cancer remains someone. You do not cross over into another realm. I was still me. I still had my home, my job, my car, my plans for the future, my family, my lover. None of these were changed by my being ill. I didn't want people to pity me or smother me with false affection, but I did intensely want to carry on as normal, live my life and look for the best.

When I decided to go back to work after the news I had made a firm resolve that so long as I was still able to do my job I would behave completely professionally and not let my private concerns get in the way.

In July of that year, about three weeks after I had received the bad news, I was working on the check-in desk as usual when a particular passenger came up to my desk. He was carrying a huge bag that weighed about 20 kilos, whereas the maximum he could carry as hand luggage was five kilos. I told him he would have to check it in.

'No,' he said. 'I want to carry it into the cabin with me.'

'I'm sorry, sir. It's over the maximum weight limit. I can't allow you to carry it on board the plane.'

He was looking aggressive by now.

'What difference does it make, whether I carry it or it's in the cargo hold?'

'Because if it should happen to fall from a storage locker. . .'

'I'm not going to put it in a locker! I'm going to carry it!'

'I'm sorry, sir. It's nearly four times over the safety allowance. You'll have to check it in.'

Suddenly he started swearing at me, calling me all sorts of names. Of course we are trained to deal with this sort of situation, how to handle troublesome passengers, so I stayed calm.

'Would you mind not swearing, sir?' I said.

'Just give me my boarding pass, you stupid. . .'

And he was off again. Now he was really angry, and a gobbet of spit came out of his mouth and flew at my face. It landed on the right side of my neck. Instinctively, I wiped it away with my sleeve.

'You deserved that!' he shouted.

I was thinking, 'How can you do this to me? How can you be so ignorant? Three weeks ago I was told I had cancer, and you think I'm only fit to be spat at.'

How could he in reality ever have known? But maybe we should all treat everyone better, just in case they are carrying around with them the sort of terrible secret I had.

No matter what, the situation had to be dealt with. All I wanted was to get him away from me. So I had an idea.

One of the alternatives we can offer passengers, if they are concerned about a piece of valuable baggage or a fragile item, is to tag the luggage and let them carry it themselves to the aircraft. Once there it has to be handed over to a member of the crew, who will place it in the fragile hold. In fact, this appalling man didn't deserve any special concessions or treatment at all, but the only thing I wanted to do was to get rid of him.

So, still keeping calm, I explained to him what I could do and what the tag would mean. I took one of the tags from my desk and bent down to attach it to the bag.

He shouted, 'Get your sticky mitts off my bag!'

He slapped my arm.

With that he finally went beyond the limit of acceptable behaviour. I asked him to calm down and to move away from my desk, and told him that I was refusing him permission to travel.

Of course, calming down was the last thing he did, and he demanded to speak to my manager. She had obviously overheard the situation blowing up and she came over immediately, listened quietly to the man's complaints, then backed me up the whole way.

He returned to my desk, leaned on the counter, bending down towards me, and breathed heavily at me in a menacing way.

What I really wanted to do was punch him on the nose. I'm the sort of person who says what she thinks, and does it too, but I was at work. We have ways of dealing with these people, and I was proud of the fact I had handled the unpleasant situation entirely by the book. I'd stayed professional and outwardly calm all the way through.

My illness, though, was making it harder and harder. I began to feel I was in the wrong place after all, that I couldn't cope any more. It's so difficult to remain professional when you're under such stress.

Some passengers can be so unreasonable. They miss

their flights, and that's upsetting and inconvenient for them, but instead of just coming to the desk and finding out if they can get an alternative flight they feel they can have a go at the check-in assistant sitting there. And they say such illogical things. One passenger demanded to know why I hadn't personally put the flight on hold, because I must have known he would turn up in the end. Another wanted to know why we hadn't called him on his mobile phone to remind him he was late.

Chapter 17

I went to see my new consultant Elaine Sugden at the John Radcliffe in Oxford. She said she was going to prepare a plan of the course of chemotherapy I should be having.

'Please,' I said. 'Is it really necessary for me to go through chemotherapy?'

'It's the most effective treatment.'

'But it isn't a one-hundred-per-cent guaranteed cure, is it?'

'Nothing is certain.'

'No,' I said. 'But chemotherapy doesn't always work.'

'It's the most powerful and effective treatment we have,' said the consultant. She could obviously read the expression on my face. 'I know what you're thinking. It didn't work before.'

'It cleared it up for a while.'

The consultant stared at the papers on her desk.

In the end she said, 'I've read up your notes, Katrina. I realize your tumour burst because of the first course of chemotherapy, and I know you suffered horribly from the treatment that followed the operation. I can tell you this, though. In the few years since your last illness, the chemotherapy drugs have improved a great deal. I'm pretty sure you won't suffer from the constant sickness.'

'It was so bad,' I said, 'that many times I simply felt that trying to recover from cancer wasn't worth the struggle.'

'Yes, I know. But believe me, things have improved.' She was trying to be as encouraging as possible. 'I feel this is the route we have to take, if there's going to be any chance of survival. We have to do that so we can be certain we tried every possibility. We want to get rid of this cancer once and for all. The first thing we have to do is reduce the size of your tumour. Then we can operate, and remove all the affected tissue. If we do it soon we should have a good chance of getting it all.'

Julian and Mum were there in the room with me.

I said to Julian, 'I don't want the treatment.'

'What are you saying?'

'I don't want it. I don't want to go through all that again.'

Earlier the consultant had told me honestly that the success rate for this kind of cancer was low, that there wasn't in fact much chance of a cure.

'Katrina, it's your only chance,' Mum said.

'Sorry, Mum. I'm not going through with it. I know chemotherapy doesn't work with me.'

I was already writing myself off, thinking ahead to how I wanted to spend the last few weeks of my life. I had always wanted to go to Australia; Julian had too. I was thinking: we could sell the house, fly to Australia together, find somewhere to live for a while, enjoy some quality time together, just the two of us . . .

The consultant listened to our conversation in silence, perhaps sensing the agony of such moments in a family's experience.

Finally, she said, 'Katrina, please do reconsider. I really sympathize with what you're saying, but think of the alternative. I'm not saying there isn't a chance for you. All I'm saying is that we can't be a hundred-per-cent sure. But we must do everything we can to give you that little chance.'

We went away to 'think about it', even though my own mind was made up. Basically, I didn't want little chances; I wanted to know that I was going to come through it.

A week later we were back in the consultant's office.

She had a medical journal on her desk, and she indicated it.

'There's been some new research in America,' she said. 'They have done a study of some people in the same position as you: adults who have suffered a recurrence of a Wilms Tumour. Out of about three hundred people this happened to, just over one hundred have survived extra treatment. There is still no such thing as a certain cure, but this evidence suggests that you have a better than one-in-three chance of survival.'

But I said, 'I'm sorry. Unless I'm certain of recovery, I don't want to go through chemotherapy again. Odds of one in three aren't good enough.'

Mum and Julian were in the room with me again, and I could feel their presence there beside me. I turned to look at them.

Mum said, 'Katrina, the last time you were ill you had no chance at all. Yet you survived. Don't you see that this is an improvement?'

'You've already lived longer than most of the adults in the study,' the consultant said. 'This suggests you must be more physically capable of fighting cancer than many people.'

Mum and Julian continued to stare at me.

It was then, when I saw the expressions on their faces, that I changed my mind.

I realized that if I refused the treatment I would be in effect killing two other people as well. I could see it in their faces, in their hearts. On the other hand, if I did agree to the treatment and it didn't work, then I would be killing only myself.

'All right,' I said. 'I've changed my mind. I'll go for it.'

I could see the relief in everyone's faces, but it was relief we shared in silence.

'You're doing the right thing, Katrina,' said the consultant.

She said she would need to see me again in a few days' time. She was going to work out how soon the treatment could begin.

We drove home from Oxford in thoughtful silence. The hugeness of the decision was looming on me, and all the effects it would have on my life.

Something really important at last found expression.

It had been on my mind from the start, but until then I had never mentioned it.

'You know this is going to ruin our wedding,' I said.

'Why should that be?' Julian said.

'Because I won't have any hair. I can't walk up the aisle when I'm bald.'

'It'll have grown back, surely.'

'Not by September,' I said, remembering the year-long chemotherapy I'd had last time.

'But some of it will?'

'No, the best I'd have would be a thin fuzz. I know how long it takes.'

Mum chimed in, 'Katrina, it'll be better than that.'

'No, it *won't*,' I said. 'I know. I've been through this so many times. As soon as they start the chemotherapy it'll all fall out, and it takes months to re-grow.'

By this time my hair had long since regained its former length, and was as golden as it had been before my first illness. Once again I was proud of my hair. It truly mattered to me.

I said, 'Mum, you know what I've always wanted.'

'A princess wedding,' she said.

'Exactly,' I said. 'But, a princess isn't bald! She doesn't have a thin fuzz of short hair. Princesses have long hair. I wouldn't feel attractive.'

'Of course you would be,' said Mum.

'No, Mum. I wouldn't. Anyway, who's to say I'll even be alive next September?'

'Katrina . . .'

'No, Mum. This is my life. What would happen if I

161

were to die? You know, my dream always was to have found the right man, settle down with him, wear my princess dress at my wedding. If I died before then, I wouldn't have died happy.'

Julian said, 'Well, why don't we get married before the treatment starts?'

'I don't see how we could do that,' I said, trying to think of all the factors involved.

Up to this point we had been planning to get married in September 1999. I wanted to have a big wedding, a proper do, and we had chosen that September to give us enough time to prepare and save up the money to be able to do it properly.

'We haven't saved up nearly enough money,' I said.

Mum said, 'Do you both really want to get married before the treatment starts?'

'Yes,' Julian said immediately.

'Then we'll make sure we have the money,' Mum said. 'Don't you worry about that. We'll find a way round it.'

When we reached home I phoned my consultant straight away.

'We've decided to get married before the treatment starts,' I told her. 'We're going to bring the date forward, and . . .'

'Katrina, we've worked out the course for you, and we've all come to the conclusion that your treatment should start as soon as possible. There's no time to lose. In fact, we've decided to start you next week.'

This was a terrible blow.

'If it starts next week,' I said, 'that's the end of it.'

'You can still get married.'

'Not the way I want to,' I replied, not willing to go into all the details. 'This is going to spoil everything.'

'Not necessarily,' the doctor said. 'Listen, there's more than one way of looking at it all. You're not going to lose your hair the moment the chemotherapy begins. There's always a short time-lag. Two or three weeks, usually.'

'That still wouldn't be long enough,' I said doubtfully.

'You never know,' she said. 'You might be able to fit it all in. If you booked your wedding for, say, three or four weeks' time. I can't promise anything. Don't take this as gospel, but it might all just work out all right.'

That night Julian and I sat down and worked out all the dates and the chances of getting the wedding in before I was in the full grip of the chemo. We sketched it out, and the next day began making enquiries.

The first problem was the church. The one we had booked for the following year was going to be closed in August for refurbishment, so that was out. In fact, that church hadn't been our first choice anyway. I had wanted to marry in the one in Milton Keynes Village. At the time they had said they couldn't marry us because we didn't live in the village.

I said to Julian, 'Look, I don't want anything to go wrong with this wedding. I want everything that we want and we won't go without. Let's try that church in the village again.'

Before we did, though, we telephoned our own local vicar and put him in the picture.

He said, 'Well, I would be happy to marry you

163

anywhere you wanted to get married. If the church in the village doesn't mind us using their church, then I could marry you there.'

With this helpful information to hand, we phoned up the village church. I spoke to Ruth Matthews, the vicar, and she too was extremely sympathetic. She suggested we should go over to see her straight away.

Once we had a chance to talk to her face-to-face we found that she was understanding and helpful. A few months earlier, when we had first starting making wedding plans, we'd run into slight objections because neither Julian nor I had been baptized. Now, though, all these problems vanished.

Ruth Matthews said that my circumstances were obviously unusual, and meant she could make a compassionate interpretation of the church's normal rules.

We decided then and there to book the wedding for 22 August. It all worked out well: not only did she still have that weekend free, but it was also the date we had reckoned would be the last possible before the chemo took its toll.

Later the same day, I went with my sister Tanya to the shop called Mignonette in Luton, which was the wedding shop from where she had bought her own wedding dress. They had hundreds of dresses to choose from. I decided that rather than spend hours going through everything and trying to find something I liked, I would simply describe what I was looking for and see what they had.

I said, 'I want a princess's dress, the sort that comes in

under the bust, goes out again at the waist. And short sleeves and a train,' I added. Suddenly I realized there was far too many in the shop to choose from. 'I just want it . . . well, princessy!'

Straight away they pulled out a dress that they thought fit my description and immediately I knew it was the one.

'I'll take it,' I said, dazed by how right it was.

'But you've hardly looked at anything,' Tanya said.

'No, this is the one.'

The assistant said, 'Perhaps you should try it on first?'

'It's right, I know it's the right one!' I said.

I tried it on, and as soon as I was inside it I was more convinced than ever.

'I'll take it,' I said.

'Why don't you try some of the others?' said Tanya. 'You can always come back to this one.'

I already knew I would be wasting time, but I tried on several more: some were what the assistant described as more affordable, and one had a longer train, but no matter what I looked at I still kept returning in my mind to the first one.

Finally the assistant told me the price. I gulped a bit, but said it was OK. The price had become of secondary importance: I had the dress I really wanted.

Neither Julian nor I had much money at this time. We had been saving towards the wedding, but bringing it forward a year had really caught us short. We discussed it and quickly agreed we'd have to take out a loan, which we eventually did. The families chipped in as much as they could too. Reed Aviation made a large collection and John Lewis had a collection too.

I was being swept along by events, and could hardly plan sensibly. The day after I picked out the dress I had to go back to hospital in Oxford for an MRI scan.

This was absolutely awful. Having a scan doesn't hurt; pain is not the problem. It's the long dark tunnel you're drawn along, the fact that you're confined in that tunnel – and the noises. The machine gives out a number of loud knocking noises which come at odd moments, terrifying you. On top of all this there's the feeling of total helplessness: you're just the human body the machine is working on, while outside, beyond your reach, is the team of doctors and technicians who can actually see what's going on.

The point of this scan was to establish exactly where the tumour was growing, what it was doing, which of my organs were being affected by it.

I was very upset when I emerged.

To cheer me up, Julian said, 'Come on. Let's go somewhere and choose our wedding rings.'

We went and looked round some of the shops, and although we saw some nice rings there was nothing we liked in our sizes. To get anything made to size required three weeks' notice. That would take us past our wedding day.

We went home without them. I was disappointed that we didn't have them. Julian had to go back to work the next day, which restricted our ability to go shopping together.

But he said, 'Look, you know the kind of ring I want.

Why not go out on your own tomorrow and choose your ring?'

All the problems of size we had met the first time we tried were caused by our wanting his-and-hers rings; I've got a small ring finger and Julian's is large. So long as we were trying to get two the same we weren't having any luck.

The next day I went out alone, and in the first shop window I looked in there were two rings I thought were absolutely right, and reduced in price too.

Inside the shop I asked the lady assistant if I could have a look at them. I put mine on and it fitted perfectly. I peered closely at Julian's, and it looked as if it was about the right size.

I made a spot decision.

'I'll take them,' I said.

The woman obviously remembered me from the day before.

'Are you sure?' she said. 'You were having so much trouble with size yesterday.'

'I'm sure,' I said. I had a feeling in my bones about it.

She looked doubtful, but she said, 'You can always bring it back if it doesn't fit. It should still take three weeks to get it changed, but we'd see what we could do to have it ready in time.'

'I don't think that's going to be a problem,' I said.

'All right.' She did a little calculation, then gave me a new price for them, fifty pounds lower than before. 'We can offer you the extra discount because the rings are ex-display.'

When Julian came home that evening I was so excited.

'Julian, I've got a present for you!' I said as soon as he was through the door.

'What is it?'

'Well, I don't know if it's going to fit . . .'

He said, 'You've bought the rings!'

The ring slipped on his finger as easily as if it had been made to measure. I knew then that it was meant to be.

Later that evening I was talking to Mum.

'Everything's working out fine,' I said. 'We've just about done all that's necessary.'

'Everything?' she said.

'All the important stuff,' I said. I was so excited. 'We've sorted out the church, the dress, the rings . . .'

'And what about the catering?' said Mum. 'And the invitations? The flowers, the horse and carriage, the reception? You want a DJ, there's the video, the photographer . . .'

'Oh yes,' I said.

Chapter 18

They had been filming at Luton Airport all through the summer, but I was wrapped up in my own concerns. I was going in to work as often as I could, and I'd sometimes catch a glimpse of them in the terminal, but I had little direct contact with them.

Then it happened that one of my colleagues was talking to the people from London Weekend Television, and she mentioned that she was going on a hen night on the Saturday evening. This was in fact *my* hen night, something that was being arranged without my knowledge. She obviously must have gone on to explain some of the circumstances.

I had only just found out about the party the day before from one of the other girls. My first reaction had been to say thanks-but-no-thanks. I simply didn't have the spare energy for a night out, however well-intended. But she had insisted, saying it was all arranged and that a lot of the girls from Reed Aviation and easyJet would be there.

She also mentioned that the TV crew would like to come along and film it.

At first I put my foot down and said no to both, but in the end I agreed to go to the hen night, but not with a film-crew in tow.

When I was at work one of the producers from London Weekend Television approached me. She told me she had heard I was getting married, and hinted that she knew the background. I told her as much as I thought I should about my new illness.

'So would you mind if we came along on Saturday and filmed your hen night?' she said.

'I'm not sure,' I said. 'I'll have to think about it.'

'OK.' She was completely unpushy, and left it at that. I immediately felt sorry I'd rejected her out of hand; she seemed nice.

Then I took a phone call from a woman at London Weekend Television. Again she was really pleasant and went out of her way to reassure me. She said the crew would like to turn up at the nightclub and film for a while, to see how I felt about having the camera on me. If I was unhappy with it at any point, all I would have to do is say so and they would stop filming immediately, and leave. She played up the positive side: she said most people were a bit nervous of the camera at first but they soon got used to it, and the majority of people actually enjoyed themselves.

We talked about it for a bit and in the end I realized they were offering so many safeguards and were in general so pleasant about it that I couldn't see what I had to lose by saying yes.

On the Saturday night, two days before I was due to

start the chemo, I went along to a nightclub called 'Chicago's' in Luton. My mum went with me, as well as my sister Tanya and my sister-in-law Suzanne. A group of the girls from work were waiting for us. They introduced us to the camera crew, who seemed a friendly lot.

When we went into the club it was obvious from the start that having a camera crew with us set us apart from everyone else. We could see people staring at us, obviously wondering if we were famous. The club were so impressed that they allocated us our own bouncer, who minded us all evening, and let us have our own private bar.

We got down to the fun, and as the lady at the TV station had promised we quickly got used to having the crew there. They were such a lovely bunch anyway, clearly enjoying themselves, that it felt as if they were part of the party.

I didn't drink much that evening, just a couple of Malibus.

At this stage the television programme was low down on my priorities, because I was in a whirl of wedding arrangements. Only the day before the hen night I'd been back to the shop to collect my wedding dress, to find myself walking into what seemed like a disaster. When I paid for the dress I had asked them to take it up to fit me because it had been far too long for me.

Now, though, when I tried it on it was too short. They'd taken it up too far. I couldn't believe it! Everything seemed in that instant to be going wrong, and I burst into tears.

The woman in the shop was very sweet about it.

'Don't worry,' she said soothingly. 'We'll sort it out in plenty of time.'

(And they did.)

All this was in one of the most hectic periods of my life.

After the hen night, one small thing had changed. The London Weekend Television camera crew were still filming at the airport and because they knew me from the hen night session, they would often come over and film me when I was checking in. I quickly got used to having the camera pointing at me.

In spite of my brave image, I was still feeling negative about my illness. Thoughts endlessly went round: about death, about fighting the illness, about surviving it, about not allowing it to get to me. I kept thinking about the light at the end of the tunnel, that little glimpse of hope that had been so important to me the last time.

On Monday, 10 August, I went to the Churchill Hospital in Oxford for the beginning of the chemo.

Unsurprisingly, perhaps, I was full of trepidation. I knew exactly what to expect, what was going to happen to me. I anticipated the constant vomiting, the loss of weight, the mouth ulcers, the fact that my cherished hair would fall out.

There was no avoiding it, though. With my heart in my mouth I went in with Mum and Julian. On an earlier visit I had taken a look round the ward I was going to be in; it was just a small one, funded by a charity. Once again I had a small room to myself.

They started the chemotherapy straight away. The first thing I noticed was the size of the bags they were using, the ones that held the fluids that dripped into me. When I had been treated before, chemotherapy was administered by injection. The injections had at least been quick; they were over within twenty minutes, but these new drips were apparently going to run all day. As everything began, as the first lines were run into me, I was half-expecting to throw up straight away.

We began early in the morning of that Monday, and by the evening it was still going on. In the end Julian had to leave to go home, but Mum stayed on with me.

The next day I had to have more chemotherapy again; this time Julian stayed the night with me.

I was feeling sick for much of the time, but by some miracle I was able to keep everything down. The staff told me that the drugs had been greatly improved over the last few years, but now I was starting to believe that it might be true. Anti-sickness was dealt with either by tablets or injections; the injections were more effective, but I had to plead for those, as they were really expensive for the hospital.

After three days they sent me home!

I was amazed: my first illness had prepared me for an extended stay in hospital, but this time they said I only needed to be actually in the hospital when the drugs were being put into me.

As I was leaving they told me they were going to give me some injections called GCSF; I never did find out what that stands for. They showed me a set of little bottles, and they said that the contents had to be injected every day. They explained that the chemo would put my immune system at an extremely low level of effectiveness, and the injections would help it to recover quickly. It was pointed out to me that they were expensive and sophisticated drugs, costing around £90 a time.

I told them I couldn't inject the drugs into myself, so they said that someone else could do it for me. Mum was there, and they showed her. For the rest of the chemo she had to administer those drugs every day, a routine we knew was necessary, and which enabled me to be at home, but which I think we both found painful, if for different reasons.

The fact that I was able to spend most of the time out of hospital meant more to me than I can say. It exactly matched my determination not to be beaten this time either by the illness or the treatment, and to carry on as close to normal as possible. This meant, emphatically, carrying on with my wedding plans, and going to work as often as I could.

I had been through cancer before; this time I was set on making the entire experience different. Therefore, as soon as I was released from hospital, I returned to work at the airport. Almost at once the London Weekend Television crew caught up with me.

I was now only a few days from the biggest day of my life: the wedding. With a week to go, the camera crew came over to my desk and asked me how I would feel about them filming the whole of the wedding. Beyond that, they wanted to build my story into the programme: the illness, our wedding, the treatment for cancer.

I said no. It was all too personal.

That night I told Julian what they had asked.

'I'm with you all the way,' he said.

'You don't want them at the wedding either?'

'No way. It's too private. It's our day.'

I was happy that we were both agreed in our decision. So my first reaction, bolstered by Julian's, was entirely negative. That seemed for the time being to be the end of it.

The next day, though, I was back at work. I watched the camera crew going about their job, filming some of the staff at work, following awkward passengers around – who for some reason never seemed to mind being filmed while they were getting into arguments and disputes!

I began to think about what it might seem like: not actually being filmed, because I'd already been through that and was used to it, but having my story shown on TV.

I wondered if it might be a practical help with my illness. Knowing that other people were going to see what happened to me might give me an extra will to live. One thing I had learnt from the last prolonged bout: to get over this illness you need all the help you can get. Not just the treatment, the drugs, the operations, but something extra, something to hang on to and something to look forward to.

At this point I had the treatment in progress, but I

also knew I lacked the right attitude. I was largely despairing of what was happening to me, was endlessly complaining to myself, feeling an extreme sense of being a victim rather than being a possible survivor.

Suddenly I thought that maybe if I had a camera following me around I would have to use my mind in a positive way. I'd have the viewers to think about, almost be answerable to them.

And then another thought. So many people equate cancer with a long, painful illness that leads invariably to death. I knew that modern medicines and medical techniques did make a huge difference. I'd already beaten cancer once, hadn't I? Maybe death wasn't the invariable outcome, and maybe this would be one way of getting that message across.

I saw myself as a creature of the TV show: Katrina, the girl with cancer, the girl who gets better. Not a story that would be just for the curious and the inquisitive, but for the hundreds and thousands of other people out there, similarly suffering from cancer, a way of getting a glimpse of my hope across to them, showing them my little light at the end of that terrible, dark tunnel.

I saw it as a great opportunity, a chance to do something useful and to get something constructive out of the illness. And the process would be two-way: it would pay me back, give me a will to live again.

That evening I said to Julian, 'You know, if I were to let them film me, I've got a feeling it might help me through it.'

'I can't see it. They're just making a TV programme.'

I told him what I had been thinking during the day, and that I was coming round to the idea.

'If you are going to be filmed,' he said eventually, 'I don't want to be involved with it. Our lives are our lives, and the whole thing is too personal to me.'

'It is to me too,' I said.

'I know that of course.'

'It'll give me something to hang my hopes on,' I said.

'What does your mum think?' Julian asked, knowing that I discuss every tiny detail of my life with her.

'The same as you,' I said. 'You needn't be involved.'

But I was thinking, 'What can I lose? What could I possibly lose?'

And I did want Julian to be in there with me.

My will to be involved with the programme was growing stronger. I talked it over with Mum one more time, then the next time I saw the producer at the airport I said she could go ahead. I wanted there to be conditions, though. I put them to her.

'I want you to film me only when I'm at my best,' I said. 'It's nothing to do with how I feel about myself. A lot of people are going to watch me, and if you film me being sick, feeling poorly, all that will do is confirm their worst fears about cancer. I have good times as well as bad. I want other sufferers to get some inspiration from me, let them know they can get through it.'

The producer readily agreed.

'We can do that,' she said. 'Listen, why don't we say that whenever we want to film you we'll phone you first and see how you're feeling? If you say no that will be it.

177

We wouldn't film that day, and we'd either wait for you to phone us back or we could phone you another day. If you still say no, fair enough.'

That seemed about as reasonable as it could be, so it was settled.

Afterwards I realized that having the camera crew behind me was one more thing on my side. You need all the psychological support you can get when you have this kind of disease. I had my family behind me, Julian, the people at work – now the TV people were on my side.

Chapter 19

We had two or three days while I was working when the crew were able to film me, but at the forefront of my thoughts, to be honest, were my two major obsessions: the illness and my imminent wedding. With less than a week before the big day, I was getting as nervous as any other young woman must feel before such an important event.

Exactly a week after I had started my treatment, I was getting ready to go into work for the late shift: from four in the afternoon until half-past midnight. I was on my own. A feeling of nausea was growing in me, and I dashed upstairs to the loo.

I leant over the toilet to be sick and without warning a gush of blood poured out of my nose. I was devastated by it.

All I could think was, 'This is the same as before – I'm haemorrhaging!'

I crouched forward over the bowl, coughing and spitting, trying to stem the bright-red flow. And in the middle of it all the telephone rang.

I grabbed a towel and wrapped it around most of my face. I made it to the telephone before it stopped ringing.

It was a former colleague of mine: my old manager at John Lewis, whom I hadn't heard from for about eight months. He was phoning up because someone had just told him about my cancer and he wanted to say how sorry he was. I could barely speak, but his call had interrupted a deepening sense of loneliness and isolation. Just to hear a friendly human voice at that moment!

But even so, I had a towel around my face, blood was splashing everywhere, and I was in no condition to carry on a conversation. Also, trying to speak only underlined the seriousness of the bleed, and within seconds I was feeling hysterical.

All I could mumble was, 'My God, I'm bleeding! I'm bleeding and it won't stop!'

The poor man, who was miles away from me at the time, tried to find out if I was alone, if I could get in touch with someone, if I needed an ambulance called, but my replies were so panicked that it was obviously impossible to hold a conversation. Finally I told him I had to go, and he put down the phone.

I phoned up my Dad because Mum doesn't drive.

I said as calmly as I could, 'Dad, I've got a nosebleed and it won't stop. What can I do?'

'I'll come over straight away,' he said.

By the time he had driven over to my house the bleeding had stopped.

I cleaned myself up as much as I could. I looked pale and drawn, but otherwise I was fine.

Dad stayed with me long enough to reassure himself that it wasn't going to start again, then had to leave to get back to his job.

I had been bleeding for about forty minutes, and as the blood dried up I convinced myself I was feeling better. I didn't want to start the hospital chasing around after me, subjecting me to endless tests, all for the sake of a nosebleed. I told myself I was fine. So I went to work, arriving late, but my appearance was obviously poor enough to attract comments. Several people said they thought I ought to go back home, but I was determined not to. I was thinking maybe it was just a little scare, that it wouldn't happen again.

I was in the countdown to my wedding, now just a few days away. On the Wednesday of that week I went to collect my wedding dress after leaving work. It brought me a surge of happiness and anticipation, because it was still as lovely as I had remembered it, and now they had made the fit right.

But I hadn't been feeling too well at work during the day, and while I was in the shop it suddenly became much worse. The next day I was even worse. I was freezing cold and shuddering, bathed in sweat. Julian was at home with me.

'I'm going to be sick, Julian!' I said suddenly. But I managed to hold it in.

'We ought to take your temperature,' he said. 'Where's the thermometer?'

'I haven't got one. The old one broke.'

He drove out to the local branch of Boots, and came

back with a new one. As soon as we got a reading from it I knew things were serious: it was 38.2 degrees.

'We're going to phone the hospital now,' Julian said.

'Don't be silly,' I said. 'I don't want them involved. It's just a temperature. If I talk to the hospital they'll say I have to go down there, and they'll keep me in.'

'Then maybe that's the right thing to do,' Julian insisted.

'We're getting married in two days' time!'

'Yes, but if you're seriously ill, Katrina, we might not be able to.'

'That's what's worrying me,' I admitted.

Just then the telephone rang. By an uncanny co-incidence it was the hospital calling to see how I was.

I took the phone from Julian.

'I'm not feeling well,' I said, 'and I've just taken my temperature. It's at 38.2 degrees.'

'Katrina, you've obviously picked up an infection and it's important we deal with it immediately. We'll send an ambulance straight away.'

'I don't need an ambulance. Julian can drive me there.'

'All right, but please leave at once. We'll be ready for you as soon as you arrive.'

I started crying as I put the phone down.

Julian said, 'What did they say?'

'They want me to come in.'

'Where?'

'Oxford.'

'No, they don't,' he said.

'They do, they *do*!' I was weeping and weeping now.

'Maybe you should go in and find out what sort of infection you have?'

'Whatever it is, they will keep me in for a minimum of five days. That's not only my wedding gone, but the honeymoon too.'

'Katrina, we must think of your health,' Julian said.

'Julian, what am I going to do?'

'I don't know.'

'Look, I've got to pack all my stuff for the honeymoon, so why don't I do that now? Then I'll be ready to leave as soon as we can.' I wasn't allowed to leave the country while I was having the chemo treatment, but my work, Reed Aviation, had booked me a weekend honeymoon in Edinburgh. 'I'll go to the hospital,' I went on, 'but it doesn't matter what they say or try to do, I'll be out of there in time for the wedding and honeymoon.'

I started moving around as quickly as I could, finding all the stuff I'd been saving up for the wedding and honeymoon, all my best gear, the lingerie, hosiery, my garter . . .

Then I thought, I'd better pack for the hospital too. That was something else, and then I began thinking that I'd need some make-up at the hospital to get me ready for my wedding.

In the middle of this the phone rang. It was the hospital.

'Haven't you left yet?' they said.

About an hour and a half had flashed by.

'I can't come over just now,' I said to them. 'I'm packing what I'll need for my wedding.'

'Katrina, please – you haven't got time to pack. Drop everything and get here now! Do you have someone there, or should we send an ambulance after all?'

'No, Julian will come with me, he'll drive me over.'

'Make sure you get here straight away. You could be killing yourself if you don't come in at once.'

In the end I finished packing, and Julian and I piled into his car with three large bags full of my stuff. We picked Mum up on the way.

On arrival at hospital I was taken straight to my little room in the ward, and at once was placed under observation. It was Julian's birthday.

He was 30, and when we had been talking to the church about the wedding rehearsal we had realized that it was going to take place on his birthday. So there I was, stuck in a hospital room, and it was the day of my fiancé's birthday, and the day of the rehearsal. I told the medical staff this.

'How am I going to get down to Milton Keynes in time?' I said.

'Katrina, don't you understand? You are seriously ill. Look at the way you're shaking.'

I couldn't deny it. I felt much worse than I had the night before. My fingers were trembling, my teeth were chattering, and I felt freezing cold. They had pumped some antibiotics into me when I arrived, but so far they had had little effect. The nurses had placed fans around my bed to try to bring my fever down.

'Surely you can let me out for my wedding rehearsal later.'

'You're far too ill, Katrina,' they said.

I expected to improve as the day went by, but by mid-afternoon I was feeling a lot worse. All I could do was lie there and tremble.

Towards the end of the afternoon Julian and Mum had to leave to attend the wedding rehearsal. They didn't want to go without me but I told them not to worry. At least they could find out what I would have to do.

I couldn't help thinking that it wasn't right. I should have been there. Even London Weekend Television were going to be there with their cameras. I was tormented by the thought of it going on without me, and in my fever I kept wondering obsessively what they were doing.

Then I remembered that I had to phone the video man. And the photographer. The people who were supplying the horse and carriage – I had to let them all know where I was, and reassure them that no matter how it looked now, or whatever anyone else might tell them, I was definitely going to be there and that the plans were going ahead. Also, I needed to confirm they all had the times right, when they were supposed to turn up, what they were expected to do. It was a mountain of organization facing me. I fretted in my hospital bed, trying to believe that it would all come right.

Later, Mum and Dad phoned to say that the rehearsal was fine, but she was very emotional, her daughter having not been there. I said I really wished I had been there.

'Katrina, it's all gone fine,' she said. 'It's going to be a lovely day. Everything's sorted out, and it will go like clockwork. We've even arranged for some chairs to be ready in the church aisle, so that when you walk up the aisle you can sit down if you need to.'

'No, please don't,' I said. 'I'm going to stand on my own two feet for the whole of that service.'

'Well, don't worry, darling,' Mum said. 'We've got it all organized.'

She kept trying to reassure me so that I wouldn't worry.

I managed to sleep on Thursday night, and when I woke up in the morning I wasn't feeling too bad at all. The nurses were talking to me and they were trying to encourage me, make me feel better about the position I was in.

They were saying they would do everything they could to get me better by the next day, but I wasn't to worry. They said I could always get married in the hospital; it's happened many times in the past.

I thought that the last thing I wanted to do was get married in a hospital.

I knew that some people might think that if I was intent on getting married, then it was the vows that really mattered. The church provided only a context for those vows, which could be said anywhere and still have the same power and effect.

A wedding day to me is something that should be memorable. It should be a happy day, looked back on as an inspiration by everyone who is there, not solely the couple who are getting married. Anyway, for my own sake I wanted a memory of that sort, not just a formal ceremony in a hospital room, speaking the vows for the sake of being married.

I also wanted to prove I could do it. It was important to me, as a signal of my intent to conquer this disease. I wanted to be good and strong in my mind, and focusing so hard on the wedding day was the best and strongest hope in my life at that time. If I showed that I was so determined to get out of hospital to marry Julian, the man I loved, at whatever risk it was to my own life, then people would understand the driving force within me.

All through that Friday I kept alternating between feeling better and feeling worse. I wasn't too bad in the morning, but I felt myself sinking a little in the afternoon. Mum and Dad kept phoning me up, telling me not to worry, they'd done this and that, they'd got the hall ready, the photographer had confirmed the times, the flowers were all sorted.

All I could say was yes, and yes, and yes. I was in a daze of hope and fear, feeling frustrated because I could not be at home getting ready for the biggest day of my life, yet still coiled around a steely resolve that come hell or high water I *was* going to be out of hospital in time the next day. Without my family, friends and Julian making all the arrangements it would never have been possible.

Finally, the doctor came to see me on Friday afternoon.

'About tomorrow,' she said, getting straight to the point. 'We think we can see a way to let you go home for the wedding, but there are a few conditions . . .'

I heard those words, and I was so excited that I barely heard the rest. I forced myself to listen to what she was saying.

'You're on a course of antibiotics, as you know, and once started that must be completed. So we've arranged for you to have them administered at the surgery in Milton Keynes before you go to the service. After the wedding service, you must come back here to the hospital, so we can complete the course here.'

'Can't I be at home for the whole day? I've got to get ready in the morning, and then after the service itself there's the reception . . .'

'No, Katrina. This is really the best we can do.'

It was something to hold on to, and something I could work on.

After the doctor had left I happened to look down at my fingernails. They were all yellow and brittle-looking. I looked in the mirror at my face and my eyebrows were all bushy. My legs needed waxing. I had been planning to do all this sort of thing on this very day, and instead I was trapped forty-odd miles from home, languishing in a hospital ward.

Sitting there on the bed I suddenly broke down again. I was feeling really ill again, but there was also the strain of pretending I was not, together with the realization I was completely unready for the next day, *and* the knowledge that everyone was at home, sorting out my wedding without me.

One of the nurses came in and found me like that, sobbing wretchedly on the bed.

She said gently, 'Katrina, we can get your eyebrows done, we can get a manicurist to do your nails.'

'In hospital?' I said between sobs.

'People come to hospitals to do all sorts of jobs for patients.'

'How am I going to find someone now?' I said.

'There must be a Yellow Pages directory somewhere. There's usually one in the nurses' station. Let's see if we can find a firm who will come out to you.'

A few minutes later she returned with the directory, and we went through it together. Within a remarkably short time it was all fixed up. Someone would come out and tidy up my nails and eyebrows.

When the beautician arrived, a new problem presented itself. My count of blood platelets was critically low again. The nurses pointed out that it was a real possibility that plucking my eyebrows could start me bleeding. One of the nurses had an idea. She put an ice-pack on my eyes, and then the beautician was able to do her work safely. After that she attended to my fingernails.

After the beautician had left I found myself on a high. A lot of my confidence had been restored. For the first time in quite a few days I was able to think: I'm getting married. I've got my wedding tomorrow! I was so excited.

I went to take a bath and to shave my legs. It was a lovely bath, hot and deep, and I lay there contentedly. I felt fine, I felt good.

After the bath I phoned up Mum.

'I'll be there tomorrow,' I said. 'Just make sure Darren

and Fenton are here to pick me up by about half-past eight, quarter to nine. I'll come to the house.'

I could hear noises in the background and I asked what was going on.

'Everyone's here!' Mum told me. 'Both your sisters are here, and Auntie Gill has just arrived, and . . .'

As she spoke I could imagine the scene in the crowded house, everyone excited and rushing around. I couldn't help being reminded that I had planned to be there too, staying the night with my Mum. It was something else I was missing out on.

Everyone was dashing around frantically, trying to get everything ready. It was all at the last minute. One of my bridesmaids, my sister Vanessa, was away at work and couldn't be contacted. Vanessa was coming to the wedding, but I had decided two weeks earlier that I would love all three of my sisters as bridesmaids, and no one had been able to tell Vanessa!

Later I telephoned work and I spoke to my manager, Sue.

'I'm sorry, Sue,' I said. 'I won't be able to go on the honeymoon you arranged for me, because they're only letting me out of here long enough to get married. I've got to come straight back in afterwards.'

She was completely understanding about it.

After the calls I was in a fine state of divided moods: halfway between being excited and high about the wedding, but also depressed because I was already missing out on so much.

I was wondering if all this illness was going to mean

that I wouldn't appreciate the day as much as I would if I was well. And because I see myself as a strong, self-reliant person, I was thinking about all the arrangements I had been going to make, and how I had let everyone else take them over from me.

Julian came down to see me on the Friday afternoon. As it happened, he turned up at a time when I wasn't feeling too well. I was lying in bed and felt so poorly that I must have looked as if I wasn't really aware he was there.

I found out afterwards that when he left he went straight round to see my mum. He poured his heart out to Mum and Dad, and said he didn't think I was going to make it to the wedding the next day. In fact, he said, he thought I was on my last legs, that I was on the point of death.

The thing was, he had never seen me ill before, certainly not the deep and traumatic illness of cancer and chemotherapy. It must have looked awful to him, as it must do to many people, but Mum had often seen me at my worst. She knew how ill I could seem, yet still pull through. Even so, she telephoned me straight away, and I was able to reassure her that although I did indeed feel lousy, it wasn't anything I couldn't handle.

When I finally turned out the lights that night I was completely unable to sleep. I tossed and turned for a while, then one of the nurses called Anne came in to see me. I talked out all my anxieties and hopes to her, as well as all the minor things that were playing on my mind. I was suddenly stricken with the thought that I hadn't brought any make-up with me, and that I wanted to wear a particular shade of eye-shadow.

She asked me what time my brothers were coming to collect me in the morning, and I told her it was about half-past eight. She said we would have plenty of time to sort all that out in the morning before they arrived, and advised me to get as much sleep as I could. She left me then, and although I was still buzzing in my mind I must have fallen asleep in the end.

The next thing I knew was that I was lying awake in the darkness and I was soaked to the skin. The bed was saturated. I put on the light; it was a quarter to four in the morning.

I was so wet I assumed at first that for some reason I must have wet myself, but as soon as the light was on I saw that the sweat was running from me. I was freezing cold, but sweating profusely. My teeth were chattering, and my limbs were shaking.

I pressed the call button. Anne came in quickly. From her expression, and the swiftness of her reactions, I realized things had taken an extremely serious turn. A doctor was called.

I heard them discussing me. I heard them talk about shock, convulsions; they looked up my medication record to discover how long it was since I had been given my last dose of antibiotics. I already knew that the antibiotics had to be administered about every five hours; I also knew by now that the doses were critical, that I was at serious risk of death without them.

The relief doctor gave me a blood test.

She said, 'I have to tell you as plainly as I can that I

think you'll be risking your life if you leave this hospital in the morning to get married.'

'It's my *wedding day* . . .'

'I know, Katrina. And I know how you must feel. But you could literally be risking your life if we let you go. Look,' she went on, 'we've had weddings in hospital before. It's not a problem for us; it can be arranged. We've got a side ward here that you can use, get your friends and family in. It's no problem.'

'What are you talking about?' I said. 'I'm getting married later today.'

'Yes,' the relief doctor said with immense patience. 'I know you are, but you must face up to the fact that you might not be able to leave hospital. Do you understand?'

'I just want to get married. I'll be fine,' I said. I was very upset.

The relief doctor said, 'Look, Katrina, I'm not your doctor and I don't have any say in what you can and can't do. Wait till your consultant comes on call in the morning and speak to her.'

I couldn't believe what I was hearing. I telephoned my dad. It was quarter-past four in the morning. He obviously knew who it was before he picked up the phone. Apparently the whole household woke up, knowing it was me.

'Katrina?' I heard him say.

'Dad, I've been advised not to get married now,' I said. 'But I am, aren't I? Please say that I am.'

'Don't worry, darling.'

'I'm at the end of my tether,' I cried. 'I don't know what to do!'

I was crying again.

'You must listen to the advice of the people there.'

'But the doctor says that if I leave hospital in the morning I'll be risking my life. Dad, you know how determined I am to get married. I'm going to be leaving here, I'm *definitely* leaving here. Just make sure that Darren and Fenton are here to pick me up at the time we planned, half-past eight or a quarter to nine.'

'Katrina, if it's dangerous . . .'

'No, Dad. I will be there at the church, I will be there!'

There was a silence.

Then he said, 'Shall I phone Julian?'

'No. I don't want Julian to know what they're saying here because I'm going to be out in time for the wedding.'

'Yes, darling.'

'It's going to be all right.'

'Of course it is.'

I tried to imagine my Dad there at home, sitting up in bed, holding the phone to his ear, forcing himself to say something. I was wondering what he really thought, whether he, like the medical staff, believed I couldn't possibly be out in time, or whether he was accepting my determination.

'Dad? Are you still there?'

'Yes, darling. You know I've never doubted your determination.'

'I've never been more determined in my life,' I said.

'OK, Katrina. We'll see you in the morning, then.'

'Yes, you will. See you in the morning.'

I put down the phone. I was still dripping with sweat, still shaking like a leaf in a gale.

Chapter 20

The consultant came into the ward on her rounds in the morning, bringing a male doctor with her. I saw them talking to another patient, and while they were concentrating on her I poured myself a glass of ice-cold water and drank the lot.

They came to my bed a few moments later, and when the nurse took my temperature they said, 'That's good – back to normal, Katrina.'

They stood together looking at my case notes. I saw them shaking their heads, conferring quietly.

'How are you feeling now?' the consultant said.

'Fine, sort of normal, really.'

'It looks as if you were extremely poorly in the night.'

'Better now,' I said.

They glanced at each other again.

'Katrina,' the consultant said. 'You know it's a matter of great concern to us if you leave hospital today to get married.'

'It's all I'm living for,' I said truthfully.

'We have all gathered that. We know how determined you are, and what a determined young lady you are.'

'I just want to marry the man I love, and do it properly,' I said.

She nodded.

'Don't worry, you can get married,' she said. 'We'll do what we can, and you'll be out of the hospital some time later this morning.'

'Oh, thank you, *thank you*!' I said. Nothing could have made me happier.

I immediately phoned up Mum and Dad, and Mum answered the phone.

'Mum! Mum!' I said excitedly. 'They've said I can come out and get married!'

'That's wonderful, darling.'

But we couldn't say much more because at that moment the two doctors returned to my room.

I put down the phone.

'Look, we think we ought to take another blood test,' the consultant said to me.

'I thought you said I was better,' I said.

'Your fever has gone down, but we ought to look at your platelets too.'

I felt a groaning sense of despair. My platelets had been low ever since I'd been in the hospital.

So they took the sample, and then I had to wait for the result.

'It's not good news,' they said eventually. 'Your platelets are so low that you could haemorrhage at any moment. I'm afraid, Katrina, this means that you can't leave as soon as we thought. Once you're out of here, we can't help you. If you were to haemorrhage, you could easily die if it wasn't caught in time. We'll have to give you a transfusion.'

I glanced up at the clock on the wall.

'How long will that take?'

'We don't have your group here,' the consultant said. 'We'll have to have them sent down by motorbike from Bristol.'

'*Bristol*?' I said in disbelief. 'But my brothers are coming to pick me up in the next few minutes.'

'We'll request the platelets straight away. I'm sorry about this, Katrina, but it's impossible to let you leave until this has been done.'

She left the ward to get the delivery in hand, and I was left to fret helplessly in my room. A few minutes later, as expected, Darren and Fenton turned up. They came down the corridor full of expectation, but as soon as they saw me their expressions changed.

'Are they going to let you out?' Darren said.

I shook my head miserably, and explained about having to wait for a transfusion.

'We'll wait,' they said. 'We'll wait as long as it takes.'

'But we haven't got all day,' I said, knowing the literal truth of that. It was my wedding day and I was confined in hospital.

The nurses were under instructions to take my temperature at half-hourly intervals, something I had not known or anticipated. One of the nurses suddenly appeared in my room to do this.

'Oh dear,' she said, looking at the thermometer. 'Your temperature's risen again.'

'Not by much, surely?' I said.

'More than it should. I'll have to tell the doctor.'

She was writing a note on my clipboard.

'But it isn't serious, is it?'

'We thought your fever had stabilized,' she said. 'This looks bad.'

When I first realized why she had come into my room, I had felt a sinking dread of what she might discover.

'But you know I've had a high temperature all night.'

'Yes, but it's risen by two degrees in half an hour.'

She re-attached the clipboard to the end of my bed.

'Look,' I said. 'I'm going to have to be honest with you. When you took my temperature half an hour ago I had drunk a glass of cold water just before. That's why it looked as if my fever had gone. I didn't want to tell anyone because I'm so desperate to get out of here.'

'Maybe,' she said doubtfully, and frowned at me. 'You shouldn't do things like that. We've got your best interests at heart.' I felt I was being given a ticking-off by a teacher, but unexpectedly she smiled a little. 'We're not keeping you prisoner here, Katrina,' she went on. 'You mustn't worry any more about having to stay in. Your consultant's made a decision, and so that's final.'

She went on to explain that all through the rest of the day I was going to have to be responsible for myself. If I felt faint, or if the fever suddenly became much worse, I wasn't to treat them as small or negligible symptoms, but to take them extremely seriously and return to hospital as soon as I could.

I said, 'I just want to be out long enough to get through the wedding service.'

'I know. I understand, I really do.'

I fretted in the room for a while longer, then suddenly there was a burst of activity. It seemed my platelets had arrived from Bristol. At the time it had felt as if they took for ever to arrive, but looking back I now realize that everyone must have moved with immense speed to get the transfusion set up for me.

The slow process began. I forced myself to relax, knowing that it could not be hurried. A drop at a time, the precious fluid flowed into my veins. While it was going on I was putting on my make-up and thinking in a worried way about my hair. I simply hadn't had a chance to make any decisions about how I wanted my hair to look.

The consultant gave me some stuff to lower my temperature.

'Right, Katrina, we want you back here by about six o'clock this evening. Seven o'clock at the very latest.'

By this time it was after midday.

'I'll get back as soon as I can,' I said evasively.

'No, seven o'clock is the absolute latest time.'

'But the reception doesn't start until eight o'clock this evening!'

She shook her head. 'I'm sorry, Katrina, you're going to have to be back here by the time I've said.'

She went on to insist that the regime of antibiotics

must not be interfered with, and explained that even though I was being released from hospital, just about the first thing I would have to do when I arrived back in Milton Keynes was to go to the surgery.

'We've arranged for your next dose of antibiotics to be administered by a GP. You must get there for half-past one.' She glanced swiftly at her wristwatch. 'The next dose is due at seven this evening. You must not miss it.'

'Yes,' I said. 'I'll do it.'

All I was thinking about now was getting out, going home, starting to get ready for my wedding.

'And we have to get you back on the drip, because you're so dehydrated.'

'Yes,' I said again. 'I do understand. I'll phone the hospital if I'm running late.'

'You mustn't be late getting back here, Katrina.'

'I understand.'

'This is serious.'

'I know.'

'All right, now you go and have a lovely and memorable day. You must really enjoy yourself.'

'Am I allowed to drink?' I said, on a sudden thought.

'If you want to have a drink, go ahead and have one,' she said. 'Keep it in moderation, of course, and enjoy yourself. The most important thing is that you must come back here as soon as you can.'

I called my brothers in from where they had been waiting all morning, and they helped me carry all my stuff down to the car. As soon as we were on our way back towards Milton Keynes I picked up the mobile and rang Mum.

'Mum?' I said. 'I've just left the hospital. I'm on my way home.'

'Really, darling?'

'Yes, I'm on my way.'

Before we hung up I asked her to give Julian a quick ring, just in case he'd forgotten what day it was . . .

Chapter 21

As we drove home Darren said that he and Fenton were starving, and he asked me if I'd had anything to eat before I'd left hospital. I hadn't eaten any food since the day before. What with all the stresses of the last few hours, the constant background feeling of sickness, and the sheer excitement of the day ahead, I hadn't even noticed.

We were driving into Milton Keynes by this time, so Darren swung into the car park at a supermarket. We went inside in search of some sandwiches.

It was while we were in there that I realized we hadn't bought any cravats for Darren and Fenton, who were going to act as our ushers. We found a tie rack in the supermarket – of course, they had no suitable cravats but they did have some gold ties. We settled for those.

When I arrived at my Mum's house I found a whirl of activity, with the house full of relatives and friends getting ready for the wedding. Vanessa was there, greatly surprised to discover what she would be doing at the wedding. There had been no time to carry out fittings on her dress, but she tried it on and by great good luck it fitted.

After some joyous reunions, the constant presence of my bandaged left arm was a constant reminder of what I should be doing instead.

Dad drove me down to the surgery in Great Holm, where my next dose of antibiotics was due on the dot of one-thirty.

I fretted again all through the treatment. I already knew that these intravenous antibiotics were a slow process, but for some reason they took even longer in the GP's surgery. Furthermore, at the end of it all I had to have the line removed from my arm, and the large white bandage needed to be replaced by a small plaster.

The whole process took much longer than I expected. At the end of it I was watching the clock nervously.

I wanted to be at home dressing and getting ready. The journey back to Mum and Dad's house seemed to take for ever.

We finally reached home by about ten past two.

I was supposed to be leaving the house at half-past two in the horse and carriage. It was already in the street outside my parents' house, with a liveried driver sitting there waiting for me. Also waiting was the photographer, the man who would be making the video – and the entire film-crew from London Weekend Television.

The house was packed inside. Several people had stayed the night, and many more had come round to visit in the morning.

The hall and the living rooms were full of flowers. I hadn't had a chance to look at them so I started to glance at the bouquets.

Mum said, 'You haven't time for that. Come and get your dress on.'

So I went and put on my lovely dress. I felt the excitement of the day starting to build up around me as I did so.

The next thing to worry about was my hair. This was a big decision, because my hair meant so much to me and I knew that within a few days I was probably going to lose it.

I had to decide how I wanted my hair to look, and staring at myself in the mirror I must admit that I became a little emotional. I knew this was quite possibly the last time I would have my hair like this, at this length, this natural blonde colour, in such good condition. I hadn't even decided how I wanted to have it for the wedding: whether to put it up so that it fitted under the veil, or to let it down. I did want people to see it, on this day of all days. Under the circumstances, it didn't take long to decide that I would let it hang down naturally about my face.

Now came the great moment: the horse and carriage were outside the house, waiting for me. With the help of my mum I went carefully downstairs and emerged from the house.

As I walked down the path, I saw the neighbours looking over at my parents' house. A surge of pride ran through me. Everyone was looking at me. I felt really special. Ahead of me, waiting in the road, was the most exquisite horse-drawn carriage, covered in flowers and ribbons. All this was for me. The horse and carriage was mine, everything in the day had been arranged as my special event.

I took my seat in the carriage, arranging the dress around me. Dad climbed in, squeezing in beside me.

'All right, my darling?' he whispered.

'I'm so happy, so happy!'

I waved to all my friends, family and neighbours watching me. I could feel the pride radiating from my father: he has four daughters but he had never had a horse and carriage for any of the others. Today we were riding in style, a special event for him as well as for me.

But this carriage had given extra worries to the staff at the hospital.

The consultant had said, 'Katrina, I know the horse and carriage are all paid for, and how much you've set your heart on being driven to the wedding in it, but we don't advise you to ride in it for the whole journey.'

'Why not?'

'How long will it take to reach the church?'

'The man said it would be just over an hour.'

'Being outdoors unprotected for so long could bring on pneumonia. In your present state of health you might not survive that.'

'I'll be all right,' I had said confidently.

'You say you will, but it's my job to protect you. Look, I've had an idea.'

She described what she wanted me to do. Because she

knew how important it was for me to drive away from the house in style, and to arrive at the church in the same way, she suggested we simply ride in the carriage for the short distances at each end. She said we could wait until we were out of sight of the house, then switch into someone's car and follow the carriage slowly for most of the rest of the way.

'That way,' she finished, 'you'd be protected from the elements and yet you'd still be able to enjoy the full effect of a grand and slow journey to your wedding.'

I had simply stared at her in disbelief, then to humour her and cut the idea short had nodded my acceptance.

Some hope! Once I was in that carriage, with everyone staring in wonder at me, nothing would have got me out again.

As we went along, Dad kept asking me if I was feeling all right.

All right? I felt like I was queen of the world!

We had some of the cars for the wedding following us, and other drivers were going past us and hooting. Drivers of cars going in the opposite direction were slowing down to have a good look. And all along the way complete strangers were waving happily to me from the side of the road and from the windows of their houses.

I told Dad I'd brought my medicines. I showed him the little posy bag I was carrying: it was filled with tablets, a thermometer, a bottle of paracetamol, sore-throat sweets.

In fact the journey to church did not take as long as we

had thought. Because I'd returned from the surgery so late, I'd had to hurry my preparations, and even so had left rather later than planned. The driver obviously knew the timing, so once we were on the main road he got the poor little horse to speed up and we rattled along at a fair old pace. I hardly had time to start feeling cold.

As we arrived at the church one of the best moments of the day occurred. I had wanted the church bells ringing, of course. No wedding would be complete without the sound of bells.

Unfortunately, this was one aspect of the wedding we hadn't been able to get right in our frantic preparations. When we had booked the church we had been told that the ringers were already booked for another church at that time on the day. It turned out that they couldn't find replacements: bell-ringing is a skilled art, and every set of bells is different. To get in replacements and train them for my day would have taken a few weeks. There was simply no time for it. Although I had been bitterly disappointed, I had had to accept that the bells would be silent. After all, everything else had been falling into place with great precision.

But on the day, on that great day, as we came into the neighbourhood of the church, I could clearly hear bells ringing. And as we got closer to the church, I realized they were ringing for me.

Later I discovered that it was London Weekend Television who had found some bell ringers, who had been trained on those bells and brought them over to Milton Keynes Village on the day.

Dad squeezed my hand.

'That's what you wanted, wasn't it, Katrina?' he said.

'Did you know about the bells being rung?'

'No, not at all.'

He seemed as moved by it as I was.

The carriage wheeled around in front of the church's lych gate, and at last I was able to descend. A small crowd had gathered, and I heard the click of many camera shutters as I stood up straight and my sisters, the bridesmaids, took up position behind me.

All the attention was focused on me and my dress, and again I felt so special.

Somewhere around me was the TV crew, working away. By this time I had grown so used to them that I hardly noticed. Certainly not that day; my mind was on many other things. We could hear the music playing inside the church but I wasn't sure whether we should go straight in or not.

Finally somebody said, 'They're all waiting for you, Katrina.'

'Here we go, then,' said Dad, tightening his elbow against where my hand was gripping it.

As we went through the main door they had to start the music again; they really had been waiting for us. How could I tell everyone I'd had to miss the wedding rehearsal, so I didn't know these things?

I found that as I walked up the aisle I was wobbly on my legs. It was difficult to take in everything. I was trying to look at everyone's faces, keep smiling, look perfect, look serene. Actually, I was feeling slightly dizzy – was it the excitement of the moment or was it a result of the illness? I made sure I smiled at a few of my close friends, and focused for a moment on the little posies of flowers that had been placed at the end of every pew.

My heart lifted.

I was here – it was actually happening!

Where was Julian? I could see his shape at the far end of aisle, standing with his back to me. Why wouldn't he turn round to see me? 'Come on, Julian!' I thought at him. 'Turn round and look at me!' I wobbled on a few more paces, then at last he turned a little in my direction, but Stuart Brown, his best man, pulled his arm as if to say he shouldn't be looking at me yet.

Finally I was there, at the top of the aisle, next to Julian. Someone had put some chairs out, and I remember thinking that I wouldn't need them: I was determined to get through this ceremony without sitting down.

But I had made it! And all I wanted to do at that moment was to go back down to the door and parade back up the aisle all over again. It had been fabulous walking slowly along between the pews, dressed like a princess, surrounded by my family and friends, all happy to see me. I could gladly have spent the rest of the day going to and fro like that.

But then the service started. My dad took my hand and squeezed it, and out of the corner of my eye I saw Julian wipe away a tear. He sometimes comes across as quite a hard person, not someone to show his feelings.

When I first knew him he hardly ever cried but now, if he feels emotional about something, he'll cry over it.

Ruth Matthews, the vicar, had started speaking.

'Welcome everybody,' she said. 'Welcome to this church for this very special occasion of the marriage of Julian and Katrina . . .'

I heard Julian gulp, and he really started crying. That made me gulp too.

Dad whispered to me, 'Do you want to sit down, Katrina?'

'No.'

All through this Ruth Matthews was going ahead with the ceremony, and I was smiling and standing close to Julian.

As the vicar was reading a psalm, Julian whispered, 'Is my nose clean?'

I couldn't believe it – he asked me if his nose was clean!

I glanced at him; his eyes were damp and he was sniffing. But his nose wasn't running, as presumably he feared it was.

'Yes!' I whispered as quietly as I could.

But when it came to the exchange of vows, Julian really broke down. I felt so sorry for him, but loved him even more for it.

When the vicar said, 'In sickness or in health . . .' we were staring into each other's eyes, and I was wondering how much Julian understood about my illness, how much he really knew and wasn't just pretending about. Even for the person closest in your life it's almost impossible to share the full extent of a critical illness.

We made it through to the end. Dad let go of my hand and Julian slipped the ring on my finger. We were pronounced husband and wife, and you could feel a wave of relief spreading through the congregation.

In the vestry, signing the register, everything felt wonderful to me. I wanted to go back and live the whole day again.

I had a feeling inside me, wishing to God that I could have appreciated this day when I was in full health. When we had been saying the vows, ''til death us do part', I had been thinking how these vows are really true because who was to say that I would be here on earth even tomorrow, or next week? Maybe God had given me this one precious day so that when I did die I would die happy. My illness put everything on to borrowed time.

This moment of thought made me realize that for the last few minutes a feeling of sickness had been growing in me, that I was not at all well. But I kept my appearance bright; I smiled, I held Julian's hand, I kissed my parents. I was going to tell no one how I felt. The prospect of the return to hospital hung over me like a shadow.

While we signed, a singer called Carole was giving a rendition of Diana Ross's 'When You Tell Me That You Love Me'; we could hear the song inside the vestry, amplified from the main part of the church, and it sent shivers down my spine.

I was determined not to cry at my wedding, though,

not if I could help it. I wanted no one to feel sorry for me, no one to feel sorry for Julian. I wanted them to feel proud of us and happy for us. If anyone saw me crying they would be sad; I wanted them to be happy, not to be sorry for me. But that song did make it difficult for a while.

We walked back down the aisle. Julian and I were side by side. He had his arm around me, all the way round, gripping me tightly under my chest. I could see by the expression on his face that he was not just happy to be married, but proud. Proud of me, proud of himself – because he had achieved a lot too.

And the cameras clicked and the videos whirred, the bells were ringing, and we clustered for photographs in the church's beautiful garden. All the way through I was receiving a silent but warm message from Julian, that we had achieved a lot together, that all that achievement had been completed and was now behind us. This was the only moment of the present we had. From this point on we were living for the future together, an unknown and probably terrifying future, but it all began here, in this garden, with our friends and family, not knowing either the worst or the best of what might come.

PART FOUR
1998–99

The Aftermath

I returned to hospital in the early hours of the morning, completely disregarding the instructions to be back by seven in the evening for my next dose of antibiotics. I had at one point telephoned the ward and told them I was fine but would be late returning; they said that so long as I was enjoying myself little else mattered. I suppose that once I was out of their sight there was little they could do but take a pragmatic line.

In fact, I was feeling far from well all through the reception, although I took care that few people would realize. All I could manage to eat was one king prawn, and I drank the toasts out of a glass containing orange juice.

Julian finally drove me back to the Churchill by about quarter-past two in the morning. The building was still and quiet. Julian and I clearly surprised the porters and night staff as we crept past them in full wedding gear.

The staff of the Blenheim Ward had laid their preparations. When we reached my little side room to the ward we discovered they had made it into a temporary bridal suite! The entrance was blocked by a strip of ribbon and inside, the room was strewn with confetti and balloons. They had pushed two hospital beds side by side to make up a temporary double bed, and there was a huge *Just Married* sign across the headboards.

They made Julian and me cut the ribbon with a pair of surgical scissors, then my new groom carried me across the threshold. It was, though, the middle of the night in a hospital, so everyone soon went away and left us to ourselves.

I had to stay in hospital for several more days while the infection cleared up, but towards the end of the week after the wedding I was allowed home. By this time my hair had started falling out in clumps whenever I combed or brushed it. I treated it as gently as possible, but there was no way of avoiding the inevitable. I phoned my mum and asked her to take me to a hairdresser, just as we had done once before. I wanted to feel that I had at least a tiny bit of control over my own destiny. As it happened, London Weekend Television were there with Mum when I called.

When she heard what I was talking about, the producer said, 'Katrina's not going to go to some back-street hairdresser. Let's take her to a top salon in London.'

They fixed it up straight away and the next day I was taken to Michaeljohn's in Mayfair. Everyone did their best to ease the process but there was no getting away from it: it was terribly upsetting, feeling my long hair being shorn away like that. I sat disbelievingly, watching myself in the mirror as the scissors did their work. I cried and cried.

The short style they gave me was certainly attractive, but it wasn't me any more. We went home and within a few more days it had all fallen out anyway. Once again I refused to look at myself in a mirror.

One evening, back at home, I caught a glimpse of myself reflected in the darkened window of my kitchen. I actually jumped in horror: I thought an alien was out there, coming to get me.

Four weeks after the wedding I went in to see my consultant, and after more tests she told me some frightening and depressing news: the chemotherapy had not had any effect at all. The tumour was as large as it had been when it was first discovered; no shrinking had taken place. The doctor said they were discontinuing the chemo straight away.

She went on to explain what this would mean, but I was hardly taking it in. I was overcome with disappointment and grief. She was telling me that in effect I had sacrificed my hair for nothing. I had gone through all the physical pain and discomfort of those powerful drugs for no good reason. All they had done was to make my hair fall out again.

Julian and Mum were there with me for this appointment. My consultant Dr Sugden was saying that we were moving straight into the second stage of the treatment: I would have to undergo a surgical operation to remove the tumour. My consultant explained that it was likely to be a long and major operation, but that every sign indicated a successful outcome. I was allowed three weeks at home to enable my body to recover from the onslaught of the chemo and to build up my strength for the operation.

On Sunday, 11 October, I went in with Julian to prepare for the surgery, which would take place in two days. You can be certain that by this time I was in a high state of nerves and not feeling at all hopeful about the outcome.

I went so far as to take Julian to one side and tell him that I was planning to write some letters which were to be read in the event I didn't pull through. One would be to him, another to my parents and a third to my little sister Janine. Julian managed to talk me out of it. He pointed out that Mum at least would interpret my writing letters as a negative sign of despair at a crucial time. She profoundly believed that so long as I remained positive and optimistic then everything would turn out all right. I knew how strongly she held this view. I also believed in it – most of the time.

However, we came up with a private way of sending personal messages into what we hoped then would be the post-operation world. Firstly, Julian and I had a bride-and-groom teddy bear set given to us by Carole, the friend of mine who had sung at the wedding service. Julian said he would take the 'bride' teddy, while I would keep the 'groom'. We would re-unite them after the operation.

Secondly, we agreed that as soon as I was conscious

after the operation, as soon as I saw that I had come through OK, I would say the words 'Juicy Lucy'. This was a family joke, based on a certain utterance of mine during a game of *Jenga* a few weeks before.

The day of the operation arrived. Mum and Julian were with me and, very early, I was given a pre-med jab and taken down to the theatre to begin the long operation. As before, the anaesthetist asked me to count to ten; I passed out before I could get to four or five. I found out later that when Julian saw me lapsing into unconsciousness he was so convinced I wasn't going to survive that he ran crying from the room. Mum had to run after him to give comfort.

Seemingly a few moments later, with no discernible passage of time, I felt myself swimming into consciousness in the recovery room, aware of people and faces all around me. For a while I was almost reluctant to wake up, so deep and untroubled had been my sleep, but fairly quickly I remembered where I was. I focused with difficulty on the face closest to me, and took a breath.

'Juicy Lucy,' I said, probably not too clearly.

The face said, 'What was that?'

'Juicy Lucy,' I said, at last being able to see what I was doing. I was looking straight into the face of my surgeon Mr David Cranston!

It was a moment of silliness at the beginning of a long period of time that was not at all amusing. As the anaesthetic wore off, and I began the slow process of recovery, I found myself in considerable and lasting pain. The surgery had been necessarily drastic and radical. As well as the tumour itself, my surgeon Mr Cranston had removed all of my spleen, half of my diaphragm – which had been replaced by a plastic prosthesis – and part of my left lung. He had help from another surgeon, Mr Quinten King. I was put on morphine for the second time in my life, and began to endure the excruciating business of post-operative recovery.

I was home within two weeks, though. Just before my birthday – on 25 October – they declared I was fit to leave. This might have been a correct medical decision, but in practical terms it was fairly disastrous. I was in a bad way: I could hardly move on my own, could not climb the stairs without Julian or Mum helping me, could barely look after myself. Once again, I was a bald, shrunken, hurting vestige of my former self. I was home, though, slowly but surely getting better, and perhaps what I appreciated most of all was no longer having to endure the rigours of chemotherapy.

Once again I had to concentrate on getting my strength back, because within six weeks I was due to start a course of radiotherapy. This had few of the physical side-effects or terrors of chemotherapy, but it did involve my attending hospital every weekday. When you consider how far I lived from the hospital in Oxford, this seemed at first to be a considerable problem. Then I came across a charity called CLIC.

CLIC stands for Cancer and Leukaemia in Children. They run a number of residential houses situated close to large hospitals, in which children and their close families can stay while their treatment is going on.

224

Though no longer a child, I was fortunate in being given a room close to the Churchill hospital, and for the duration of the radiotherapy I moved in.

The actual radiotherapy treatment is carried out remarkably quickly. You are exposed to the stream of highly focused radiation for just a few minutes. The business of positioning your body in the correct place on the apparatus takes longer than the radiotherapy itself. A typical treatment would last about twenty minutes. However, I was not allowed to miss any of the sessions and although the side-effects, compared with those caused by the chemo, were mild, they still had to be endured. I always felt sick after the treatment, and every afternoon between three and four o'clock I'd fall asleep for a couple of hours.

I was allowed one extended break over Christmas of 1998 – our first Christmas as husband and wife. I couldn't help remembering the last time I had spent Christmas with the shadow of cancer hanging over me. But it was great to be back with my noisy, happy family. Everyone turned up for the party – all my brothers and sisters, the in-laws, my nieces and nephews – and there seemed to be no forcing of the sense of fun. They kept saying the same thing to me: the worst was over, everything was going to be all right. I don't know how Mum coped with it all: she hadn't had much chance to get ready, so she was rushing round right up until the last minute on Christmas Eve. It didn't stop Dad dressing up as Father Christmas, though.

Three days later, on 28 December, I returned to hospital to conclude the course of radiotherapy.

By the middle of January 1999 it was all over and, apart from periodic check-ups in the months and years to come, to make sure the cancer is not returning, my treatment was at an end.

I wanted to return to work as soon as possible, because I saw it as the quickest route back to normal life, but we had at last been able to book our postponed honeymoon in Edinburgh. Reed Aviation encouraged me to take the holiday first, before returning to work.

We went away for Valentine's Day weekend, in February. London Weekend Television were there at Luton Airport to film Julian and me as we boarded our plane. By this time, the *Airline* programme was going out every week, and they were just able to film me in time to slip our departure into the last show.

Of course, the effect of the programme going out had not fully sunk in at the time, but when we arrived in Edinburgh the Press were there to greet us. The episodes leading up to our wedding had been going out – now here we were, arriving for our honeymoon. I imagine they had only the faintest idea of what had been going on in the intervening months.

After the honeymoon life returned gradually to normal. I went back to work at Luton Airport in March, and after a disconcerting lack of recognition when I first went into the office – I had lost over a stone in weight – I was given a hero's welcome by my friends. I enjoyed that.

I was soon back on the check-in desk, dealing with the passengers and their numerous concerns. They at least had not changed: most of them were terrific to deal with, but as ever a few of them seemed determined to be as nasty as possible.

The first time it happened I retreated to the office in tears, thinking, 'I can't take this any more. This is it – I'm leaving, my career has gone out the window.' The second time was even worse. But something made me put a smile back on my face: the TV crew followed me in and, although I wasn't frightened to show my feelings in front of the camera, the presence of the crew reminded me of what I had originally intended.

I didn't want other cancer sufferers, who might watch the programme, to see me having a bad time and apparently being defeated simply because I had been ill. Having the crew there actually gave me strength, made me sort out my priorities. I realized, after all the agonies I'd been through, that being shouted down by someone because a plane was ten minutes late taking off was no longer an option. I knew I could not walk away from such a situation. It made me a lot stronger, but there is of course a price to pay.

I always make sure that whenever the cameras are on me I come across as the happy, bubbly Katrina they first discovered. Deep down, though, I have a lot of bitterness inside me. I still wonder why this happened to *me*, when there are so many wicked people out there in the world enjoying full health. But I've learnt that this is a feeling many cancer-sufferers share, that in a sense it goes with the territory. I'm learning to fight the feeling, to accept that cancer is not some kind of retribution for past sins. It strikes and it strikes randomly. It has to be borne by those who are stricken. Needless to say, I wonder endlessly if the cancer will return, if all the pain and suffering is truly behind me ir if I will have to go through it all again.

I hope and intend to give faith and inspiration to other cancer sufferers. It's only natural, though, to wonder if I'm going to become ill again. The best way I can deal with this fear is by maintaining a positive appearance, by being as bright and cheerful as I used to be and hope that this will lead eventually to a return of the real Katrina.

No one, except perhaps Julian and my closest family, knows how easily things get me down these days.

I feel I have finally conquered the problem of coping with awkward passengers, and can handle them professionally and calmly if they decide for whatever reason to have a go at me. I know that the rest of my life can follow from the example of this clear step forward, that it's only a matter of time.

The hardest thing is to put the fear behind me: I remain free of cancerous cells, but every new check-up looms up terrifyingly ahead of me. It will be years before I'm able to put this fear into greater perspective. Even so, I have been free of cancer for a year, and my body is rapidly recovering from the traumatic effects of the treatment, of the chemotherapy in particular. My hair is growing back, and most of the time the smile I put on for the benefit of the world is not forced.

With the television series taking my story out into the

world I have had to adjust to the effects of becoming a person many people recognize and think they know. Some of that, as I have said, has caused temporary problems, but now that the second series of *Airline* has been recorded and shown I realize that overall the effects have been beneficial.

And not only beneficial for me. I've had masses of letters from people who have seen the show, and it's obvious that they have gained something from my experiences. Two Australian viewers on a visit to London made a special trip out to Luton Airport just to meet me and tell me what an impact the programmes had had on their lives. Another man, a prisoner in one of our gaols, wrote to say how upset he had been that someone as innocent as me should be struck down by cancer while he, a criminal, remained in good health. He told me that as soon as his sentence was completed he was going to make something of his life.

My long-term plans are straightforward and easily stated. At the moment I want to stay working in the airline business, perhaps moving up into management. More importantly, perhaps, I hope that one day Julian and I will be able to have a family.

I come from a large, happy family. My mum had six children and that seems like a reasonable target for me to beat. I'd settle for seven.

But at the moment the medical verdict on my having children is not clear. All they will say is that when we want to make actual plans I should speak to my doctors. The chemotherapy and radiotherapy have put a great strain on my body, and it might be difficult for my heart to withstand the various stresses of pregnancy.

If I were not able to have children the disappointment would be terrible to bear. All I can do at the moment is try to prepare for that disappointment, harden myself against the idea of having children. It's a self-defensive instinct. I've had so many unwelcome shocks in my life that I'm trying to learn how to anticipate them. I'm building up a barrier against pain to protect myself. I prepare for the worst that can possibly happen, while hoping for the best that might.

If I have an example to give to fellow cancer-sufferers it is that they must have something to look forward to. I always saw this as a light gleaming at me from the end of the tunnel: something to which I made myself press forward.

You must invariably look to the future, prepare for it, plan for it. Cancer can be beaten, and there is life and hope beyond that moment when you are told the worst news in the world.

I have lived that moment twice, and I do not ever want to live it again. But against that terrible possibility I am building inner resources of strength, and beyond those I continue to make my plans for the future.